CASE STUDIES IN
EDUCATION AND CULTURE

General Editors

GEORGE *and* LOUISE SPINDLER
Stanford University

THE SCHOOL AT MOPASS
A Problem of Identity

AREA OF THE
YUKON INDIAN AGENCY

THE SCHOOL
AT MOPASS

A Problem of Identity

A. RICHARD KING

Teachers College, Columbia University

HOLT, RINEHART AND WINSTON

*New York · Chicago · San Francisco · Atlanta
Dallas · Montreal · Toronto · London*

Foreword

About the Series

This series of case studies in education and culture is designed to bring to students in professional education and in the social sciences the results of direct observation and participation in educational process in a variety of cultural settings. Individual studies will include some devoted to single classrooms, others will focus on single schools, some on large communities and their schools; still others will report on indigenous cultural transmission where there are no schools at all in the western sense. Every attempt will be made to move beyond the formalistic treatments of educational process to the interaction between the people engaged in educative events, their thinking and feeling, and the content of the educational process in which they are engaged. Each study will be basically descriptive in character but since all of them are about education they are also problem-oriented. Interpretive generalizations are produced inductively. Some are stated explicitly by the authors of the studies. Others are generated in the reader's mind as hypotheses about education and its environmental relationships.

The cross-cultural emphasis of the series is particularly significant. Education is a cultural process. Each new member of a society or a group must learn to act appropriately as a member and contribute to its maintenance and, occasionally, to its improvement. Education, in every cultural setting, is an instrument for survival. It is also an instrument for adaptation and change. To understand education we must study it as it is—embedded in the culture of which it is an integral part and which it serves.

When education is studied this way, the generalizations about the relationship between schools and communities, educational and social systems, education and cultural setting that are current in modern educational discussions, become meaningful. This series is, therefore, intended for use in courses in comparative and overseas education, social foundations and the sociology of education, international educational development, culture and personality, social psychology, cultural dynamics and cultural transmission, comparative sociology—wherever the interdependency of education and culture, and education and society, is particularly relevant.

We hope these studies will be useful as resources for comparative analyses, and for stimulating thinking and discussion about education that is not confined by one's own cultural experience. Without this exercise of a comparative, transcultural perspective it seems unlikely that we can acquire a clear view of our own educational experience, or view education in other cultural settings without ethnocentric bias.

About the Author

A. Richard King's first contact with Yukon Indians was unintended. It came as a result of an ill-fated attempt to establish a new bush airline in the north country of Alaska and the Yukon Territory. King and his two partners lost their plane and equipment when they crashed in Teslin Lake, Yukon Territory, en route to Alaska from the United States. Rescued by a Royal Canadian Mounted Policeman and Teslin Indians, the three young Americans spent six weeks in the Indian village, which was the only habitation along Teslin Lake. At that time the Alaska Highway was an "impossble dream," and Teslin was one of the more remote portions of the Territory. Only the policeman and a trader were non-Indian residents of the village. The trading post manager, an amateur anthropologist and expert on Yukon Indians, provided King with initial understandings of both the Indians and anthropological perspectives.

Today, a quarter of a century later, Teslin is a thriving Highway city in the Yukon Territory. Some of the children mentioned in this publication are members of families King knew in 1939.

After wartime experiences in the United States Merchant Marine and the United States Marine Corps, King was graduated from Western Washington College, Bellingham, Washington, and became an elementary school teacher in Washington state. In 1949 he went to Saipan to teach in an armed forces elementary school for a year. He remained in the islands of the Trust Territory of the Pacific (Islands) for the next five years, teaching and administering the development of the native elementary schools in the Saipan, Truk, and Ponape districts. This period further developed King's interest in applied anthropology and its relevance to educational administration and educational assistance programs. The results of the Coordinated Investigations of Micronesian Anthropology (CIMA) were becoming available at that time. The leadership and guidance provided by Homer G. Barnett and Frank J. Mahony, staff anthropologists in the Trust Territory of the Pacific Islands administration, were particularly significant influences upon King's career.

From 1956 through 1960 King taught and was an assistant to the superintendent of a suburban school district in Edmonds, Washington, while he continued part-time graduate study in school administration and sociology at the University of Washington. In 1960 he became a doctoral student in the Stanford University Comparative Education Center, which is under the joint direction of Paul R. Hanna and George D. Spindler. His major fields of study were education and cultural anthropology. In 1964 he was granted the Ph.D. degree at Stanford.

Since 1964 King has worked as an associate for international development with a forty-man team from Teachers College, Columbia University, which is assisting the development of teacher education systems in Afghanistan under a USAID contract. In 1966 King became associate chief of this contract party, with specific responsibility for coordinating research activities in Afghanistan and for coordinating the participant training program for Afghan students in the United States.

King's writing includes the first elementary curriculum guide prepared for district elementary schools in the Trust Territory of the Pacific Islands; a study of a nongraded elementary school in Edmonds, Washington; bibliographic annotations for the Stanford Research Institute publication *Human Resources and Economic Growth,* a framework for research and evaluation of educational assistance activities under the TCCU/USAID contract in Afghanistan; and text materials for courses in social science and sociology offered at Kabul University's Faculty of Education.

About the Book

This book describes the educational process in a residential school for Indian children in the Yukon Territory of Northwest Canada. It is a case study of how children learn the subculture of the school and how, in this process, the intended aims of education, as enunciated by teachers and school administrators, are defeated. It is a study of how children learn to cope with an adult-made social and semantic environment: how they learn a pragmatic gamesmanship that makes it possible to get along in that environment; but how, in winning the game, often to the confusion of the teacher, the children lose. It is a study in communication and in noncommunication—among children, between teachers and children, and between administrators and teachers—in a closed educational and social situation. It is a study of roles and how these roles interact to reinforce mutual stereotypes. It is a study of acculturation, of the attempts of an indigenous minority group to move into full participation in Whiteman[1] society, and of why these attempts fail.

This book discusses intriguing and significant questions: How does learning the culture of the school, in both its classroom and peer group discussions, make it difficult for the Indian child to operate effectively in the outside world? Why do the children of Mopass Indian Residential School lose interest in learning about the time they are in their third year in school? Why do children avoid making decisions, and thus manifest behavior that confirms adult non-Indian views of Indian children as incapable of learning to make decisions? Why do Indian children rarely take initiative in seeking affection from even kindly and well-disposed "Whiteman" adults, although they feel a deep need for it? Why are there several orders of reality for Indian children? Are Indian children capable of the same kind of academic achievement as White children?

The author discusses these questions and the relevant evidence with objectivity. He never takes the view that simply the teacher is at fault, but shows how forces are set in motion by the situation and its definition, which are impersonal, disinterested, and apparently irreversible in the present context. Although this is a case study of one educational institution in one setting, it is apparent that the situation of all racial minority groups of relatively low socioeconomic status in North America is represented. The self-reinforcing processes, in the Yukon Territory as elsewhere, lead to segregation, to low educational and economic achievement, and to nonparticipation in the dominant society, and the rewards of these processes, constituting a massive and tragic scab in our society, are represented here in microcosm.

---

[1] "Whiteman" is used in this case study as a term designating members of the dominant society as contrasted to Indians. It is the most frequently used Indian term for this purpose and includes *all* non-Indians generically. It is not pronounced as two words; it is more nearly spoken as is the name of the well-known orchestra leader Paul Whiteman. (See also p. 3.)

Students of minority group education, of the education of the alienated and non-participating, of the culturally disadvantaged, will find much of value in this case study. Students who are interested in the analysis of acculturation process and of cultural transmission, will also find much to intrigue them.

George and Louise Spindler
General Editors
STANFORD, CALIF., 1967

Preface

This case study results from the initiative of Lyman Jampolsky, Superintendent of Education for the Western Region (British Columbia, Yukon Territory, and part of Alberta), Indian Affairs Branch, Canadian Bureau of Citizenship and Immigration. In 1962 Superintendent Jampolsky came to Stanford University, among other places, seeking anthropologically trained teachers for the Indian schools in his region. He said he felt that a series of case studies by trained participant-observers would lead to a better understanding of the multitude of personnel problems, involving both students and teachers, and of the seemingly static operation of the Indian schools.

He described the Indian school situation as one where the best of intentions operated and at least *some* very good people worked, but for all of that, one whose undeniable outcome is that Indian children ". . . are not being reached": The children are not staying in school beyond the required ages—and often not that long; they are not changing from their traditional "bush" orientation to participation in the progressive Canadian development that surrounds them. In short, the Superintendent described a system that is dysfunctional in the sense that it does not produce the kind of product which it is intended to produce. The desired "product" might be defined as a well-integrated Canadian citizen equipped with attitudes and intellectual skills that enable him to function within the larger society in basically the same manner as other citizens.

At the time Superintendent Jampolsky came to Stanford, the author had completed his graduate studies and was considering prospective sites for a year's field study of a cross-cultural educational situation. Lengthy discussions and reviews of the literature (which was scanty, at best) culminated in his being one of three who agreed to spend a year in the Indian schools as combination teachers and participant observers. For the author, this profitable year resulted in a doctoral dissertation (King 1964) and in this case study.

Despite how the study came about, however, it must be made completely clear that the observations and conclusions are totally the responsibility of the author and in no way are to be construed as reflecting the either official or unofficial opinions of the study's sponsors. Because of the sensitive nature of some of the material and its pertinence to the work and career relationships of those who are in the Indian Affairs Branch, the author has reluctantly refrained from even presenting copies in advance for examination and comment. All names and places in this book are fictitious. In some instances, characterizations are composites rather than true descriptions of individuals. In all cases, however, situations and personalities are "true" in the sense that they exist in the relationships and patterns indicated.

To Superintendent Jampolsky and to all the many others of the Yukon area who were such gracious hosts and who so willingly assisted the author, deepest appreciation is extended. The author also wishes to acknowledge his indebtedness to Charles C. Hughes, who read and criticized an earlier version of this case study, and to George D. Spindler, who has acted as a supportive critic during the research and the writing up of the results.

A.R.K.

Kabul, Afghanistan
September 1967

Contents

Standardized Tests and Their Implications, 83
Summary of the School as a Learning Environment, 86

THE SCHOOL AT MOPASS
A Problem of Identity

A view of Mopass and adjacent lake and mountains. The station side of the river is Whiteman housing; across the river (not shown) is Indian housing—no Whitemen live there.

Introduction

THE YUKON INDIAN AGENCY provides a relatively simple, straightforward setting for a study of modern Indian-school operation. The variables that operate, and have operated in the past, are probably as limited as anywhere in the history of Whiteman²-Indian contact. In the total contact history of this region there has been no armed hostility. The Indians of the Yukon have not been displaced from choice lands or confined on reservations. No treaties have been involved. Without direct external force being applied, Yukon Indians have tended to abandon their traditional subsistence patterns in favor of settlement in or near the towns of Whitemen, adopting the Whiteman's housing patterns, his food, his religion, his naming system, his language—all with minimal adaptations. Indeed, the Yukon Indian almost eagerly abandoned whole sets of traditional patterns and sought maximum identification with the new and dominant society *up to a point*. At that point, a social position implicitly defined by the Whiteman rather than by the Indian, the tendency toward fusion stopped, and the Indian found himself in somewhat of a limbo world from which he has not escaped. Little of his traditional society remains to provide him with identity, and all but impenetrable barriers keep him from realizing a satisfactory identity within the dominant society.

Although the Yukon Territory of Northwestern Canada is one of the lesser-known regions of North America, it is far from being an isolated region bypassed by national development. The Government of Canada is giving increasing emphasis to the development of its vast northern region, rich in both natural and human resources. Along with the Northwest Territories, the Yukon Territory comprises one of the most dynamic, rapidly expanding areas of Canada into which tremendous investments of money and effort are annually expended.

As a single, not atypical illustration of the level of investment in recent years, a little more than $1275 per pupil was spent for Indian education in the fiscal year ending March 1961 in the Yukon Territory (Government of Canada 1961). This sum does not include capital outlays for plant facilities and is a large per-pupil expenditure in any school system anywhere. Official Canadian policy at all levels reflects the intent to provide the best possible education for the Canadian Indian population. Yet this enlightened policy and the adequate investments have not significantly changed the Indian population from one that is economically and so-

---

² See footnote 1, Preface.

cially peripheral. Yukon Indians are neither independent of, nor a part of the dominant society.

This case study deals with a single residential school in the Yukon Indian Agency. It is one of fifty-nine similar schools in Canada. How and why is such a school established? Who operates it?—In what manner? And for whom? With what results? Quick answers to these questions serve only to focus upon the dimensions of the problems and to justify more intensive examination.

All Canadian Indian residential schools are operated by churches under contract to the Canadian government, which pays all costs, including the salaries of classroom teachers who are civil service employees. All the schools take beginning students at six or seven years of age (or older), but the top grade levels vary according to local government policies and the facilities available. The school at Mopass has reached a near-optimal situation (with "optimal" defined as "total integration"). Upon completion of grade four at the residential school, Indian children transfer to public schools in the capital city, Whitehorse, where they live in a government-operated hostel and continue to receive full subsistence as long as they remain in school. The Mopass School serves only Protestant children, as does the hostel in Whitehorse. A similar residential school and a similar Whitehorse hostel exist for Catholic children. Between them, the two residential schools serve a majority of the Yukon Indian population, although a number of Indian children live at home in the various towns of the Yukon and attend local public schools. Most of the adult Indians in the Yukon today have attended residential school at one time or another in their lives. Permission for Indians to enroll in regular public schools is a relatively recent development, one initiated only after World War II.

About one fourth (2870) of the Yukon Territory's total population is legally designated Indian. Many others, Indian by birth and heritage but legally "enfranchised" (a term that will be more fully explained later), raise this proportion of the total population to one third. Of this number, fewer than 10 have been graduated from high school (grade twelve); none, from any university. In 1962, the age group of sixteen to twenty-one years included 156 persons. Of these, 127 had quit or been dismissed from school; twenty-nine were still in school. None of the 127 had been graduated from high school; only twenty-seven had gone beyond grade eight while twenty-eight had not passed grade six. Forty-seven girls of that age group had children in 1962; twenty-six of these girls were not married when their children were born.

At the same time among the adult Indian population, fewer than a dozen were employed at any work on a full-time basis. Some form of government-supplied social welfare or benefit fund provided the total family money income for 182 separate claims, 127 of which were "permanent assistance" directly from the Indians Affairs Branch.

Such a brief review of statistics, taken directly from the Yukon Indian Agency files (with the courteous cooperation of agency personnel), illustrates the meaning of comments about the "product" of Indian schools not functioning within the larger society in the same manner as other citizens. While there are elements of school dropout, unemployment, and permanent or semi-permanent welfare depen-

Children of the fourth grade, Mopass Residential School, and the author during a midwinter walk on the lake in front of the school.

dence among the non-Indian population, the number of cases among non-Indians is negligible in comparison with that among Indians. The non-Indian population of the agency region is essentially prosperous, middle-class Canadian. Clearly there are fundamental differences between the Whiteman and the Indian populations which result in Indian deviance from the expected educational patterns and in Indian marginal socioeconomic status.

Since a majority of the Indian children spend most of each year of their early schooling in the residential institutions, it seems reasonable to examine this experience as a possible source of their attitudes, values, and observable performance. In terms of time available in which to exert an influence, the residential school has a five to one (ten months to two months) preponderance over home and family.

After a brief description of the setting, we shall look closely at one family that has provided children to the school at Mopass. In this diverse and limited population, we shall not try to establish a "typical" family, but shall merely point out that the Mathews family contains most of the elements of most Indian families in the Yukon: a successful entry into Whiteman society; several failures to effect such entry and a deliberate rejection after partial success is achieved; ambivalence about identity, integration, and family solidarity; loss of language and of other basic cultural traits along with a reaffirmative clinging to a few persistent memories and patterns; limited goals and limited means for achieving goals, especially among the young. We shall then conclude Chapter 1 by examining the broader social context in which the residential school operates.

In Chapters 2 and 3 we shall look intensively at the school itself—at its operation and facilities, its personnel, the relationships that prevail among adults and children during a normal year of operation, and the performance of pupils in classes. Finally, we shall identify some of the critical areas in this situation which might provide a possibility for a breakthrough in the cyclical pattern, although the function of this study is analytic, not prescriptive.

It should be remembered that all the processes in this case study are described as they were observed in 1962–1963. Many changes will have taken place since that time but the underlying patterns of behavior, beliefs, and interactions should continue to be recognizable for a long time. The author's specific role in the residential school was that of senior teacher. Formally ascribed role behavior for this position combines minor administrative duties, instructional staff leadership, and full-time teaching. Informally, the position requires a complex set of role behaviors that introduce unavoidable bias into the total situation and into observations. The senior teacher is "boss" to some, "friend" or "coworker" to others; he is neutral in certain situations, threatening in some cases, supportive at other times—all depending upon many personality and situational variables. The information presented in the following pages is factual as observed or related to the observer, with personal idiosyncrasies avoided except where they reflect significant aspects of social and cultural processes.

1 / The school community

A LL YUKON INDIANS except the Tlingit and Tahltan in the extreme south speak in languages classified as Athapascan (Osgood 1936). Local variations make communication in the native language increasingly difficult as distance between groups increases. Southern Yukon Indians say they ". . . don't understand" central or western or nothern speech. The use here of the present tense, "speak" is a historical present; few people other than the very old still communicate with one another in the native language, and few children are able to use the native language at all. A sparse, almost pidgin English in uniform present tense, with many omissions of "to be" verb forms and few modifiers, is the most usual form of communication among these Indians.

The Yukon Indians' reported degree of lack of understanding among themselves may reflect a lack of *desire* to understand more than it does any lack of ability to do so, and lends some support to the theory of at least one anthropologist that the entire population inhabiting the interior basin at the time of Whiteman contact was wiped out by either disease or internal conflict and has been replaced by newcomers from what was at one time the periphery of the region (Jenness 1957). Although no direct evidence is available in anthropological or historical literature, it seems almost certain from present evidence that the Yukon Indians either have experienced major acculturation stresses from contacts with other Indian groups or are scattered remnants of displaced Indian groups who originated elsewhere.

Within the drainage area of the upper Yukon River, from the Alaska border to the headwaters of the Yukon, few adults can trace their ancestry by name beyond the third ascending generation. Most of them do not use any tribal designations in reference to themselves or their people. The only exceptions are the Kutchins, far to the north (and, in 1962, outside the Yukon Agency), and the Tahltan and Tlingit, far to the south. At one earlier period, Kutchins were more numerous—possibly dominant—but today there remains only one small band, from which only an adventurous fraction ever move as far south as Whitehorse for any reason (Balikci 1963). Tlingit bands of the southwest Yukon trace their origins directly to the Pacific-slope Tlingit of the area around Juneau, Alaska. Their immediate ancestors were undoubtedly the Tlingit entrepreneurs who penetrated the Yukon Basin in order to trade Whiteman goods for furs, following initial—probably Russian—contacts (Krause 1848). Tahltans of the Yukon Agency actually lived in northern British Columbia and are included in the agency solely for administrative convenience. Only a few rejects from the home community ever get into the Yukon Territory itself.

Such historical possibilities must be the subject of other studies. Here, the significant facts are that to the Yukon Indians identity is a very real problem. No heritage of cultural unity exists to provide identity linkage for Yukon Indians which might be analogous to that among the Navajo or Blackfoot, for instance. Yukon Indians are a heterogeneous, highly individualistic population. They have shared a common, traditional life cycle of seminomadic hunting and gathering subsistence; a common technology dictated largely by the environment (that is, snowshoe types, uses of skins and furs, fauna, bone, stone, wood); and a basic language structure. Otherwise, they have few common denominators among themselves other than a common relationship with the Whitemen.

Whitemen euphemistically speak of the "Indian community" when they wish to refer generally (and politely) to Indians as distinct from Whitemen. For administrative, welfare, and legal purposes, Indians are defined as those whose *fathers* were legally Indian (that is, not enfranchised) as of a given date, or whose mothers if unmarried, were Indian. No degree of "Indian blood" is used as a criterion for identification, and there is considerable official confusion about some Indian identities, especially where multiple marriages or no marriages have taken place. (The confusion does not extend to social relations; Whitemen identify Indians by preformed stereotypes of appearance and behavior, not by legalisms.) Many people in the Yukon who could qualify as "full-blooded" Indians have chosen to become enfranchised. This amounts to acquiring full rights as a Canadian citizen by renouncing claim to Indian identity. It was most frequently done in order to acquire rights to purchase liquor prior to 1963; in that year all Indians were granted this right whether they were enfranchised or not. On the other hand, nearly all legal Indians have some degree of non-Indian ancestry in the preceding three generations.

In reference to the school children of this study, the term Indian is used in its strict legal sense, since non-Indians are ineligible for the type of support or facilities offered to Indians. In reference to Indian families and attitudes, however, this distinction is not possible. Persons of Indian ancestry invariably identify themselves as Indian, regardless of their legal status and are never heard to refer to themselves as Canadian.

All legal Indians are also required to identify themselves by religion, and this is a much more functional identity. Catholic Indians are positive in their assertion of faith; Baptists, Anglican, Pentacostal, B'hai, and other non-Catholic sect members are equally positive in the assertion of Protestantism.

The traditional life pattern of Yukon Indians, both before and for many years after the Whiteman came, involved annual cycles of seasonal movement from lake to lake or to river, movements determined by the habits of the animals, the quantities of fish, and the ripening of the few fruit and vegetable crops that flourish in the scanty northern "bush" country (taiga). The primary economic unit was the monogamous nuclear family. Often, two or three related nuclear families cooperated in large tasks while maintaining separate households.

The movement cycle took place within a bounded area, usually a drainage pattern including a series of streams and their inlet or outlet lakes. One or two of the lower and best fish lakes would be the winter camp site each year. Major movements took place for spring and fall hunts, for berrypicking, and for trapping. Between migrations visits to other camps provided a loose system of grapevine communication and sustained a pattern of expected hospitality and reciprocal giftgiving. This loose linkage bound the population at least in awareness of one another, although it was not infrequent that related adults would see each other only after a lapse of several years.

Certain older men were known as persons who could ". . . tell you what the right way was." These men were consulted more frequently than others for advice in the settlement of disputes. Otherwise heads of families, or the eldest of a multiple family group, were the authorities. No concept of "chief" or formal hierarchy outside the family structure was involved.

The geographic areas of family or family alliance groups were considered property in the loose sense that intrusion by outsiders for the purpose of competitive utilization of the same resources was resisted or resented. However, no clear definition of landownership was needed. The Yukon has far more drainage areas than have ever been inhabited or completely utilized. Competition for specific land rights was probably rare; aside from occasional minor conflicts about overlapping trap lines, the reminiscences of old people do not contain mentions of land conflicts. Even today, when the Yukon is surveyed and owned either by the Crown or private individuals, plenty of land is available for anyone who wishes to resume the traditional hunting- and gathering-pattern of living. One elderly Indian man said, "Give me a good woman and any five-mile square of land around here and we could live well and make a couple thousand dollars a year cash to boot. But who wants to spend their lives out in the bush? Our people don't want to live like that no more. . . ."

From the first contacts Indians of the Yukon seem to have tried to accommodate to the ways of Whitemen, whose technological skills and equipment were obviously superior and whose social organization seemed an obvious improvement. The Indians' initial contacts were with the traders and missionaries who followed closely behind the explorers of the eighteenth century. These mutually supporting groups brought a welcome increase of material goods and introduced Christianity. Since the Whiteman's religion seemed an essential prerequisite to participation in his other activities and since the native religion included no formal organization and little ritual or ceremony, Christianity met with little resistance. Indeed, competition between Catholic and Protestant missionaries in securing and keeping converts was probably the source of more factionalism and conflict than competition between Christianity and any native religious element. But even this conflict probably did little more than replace other antagonisms, antagonisms that had been more random and not so well defined. Christianity seems to have been generally welcomed by the Indians for the supportiveness and social-control mechanism it offered. Early missionaries were always a source of food and medicine or assistance in emergencies, including intercession with other Whitemen in puzzling situations. The church offered a birth-to-death set of ceremonies with prescribed rituals and hierarchical statuses into which Indians were accepted at least up to specified levels. An Indian baptised, confirmed, married, and otherwise recognized in a given church could be assured of acceptance among a wider group than in his traditional non-Christian society. No Yukon Indian has ever held a government office or an important civic post, but many have held recognized offices in churches, some even being deacons and lay ministers.

The first two or three generations following contact and the arrival of traders and missionaries effected a real movement toward development of a homogeneous society in the Yukon. A first big step for the Indians was baptism, a ceremony that promised true identification because it involved the taking of a Whiteman name. Along with the names, the Indians accepted the Whiteman's way of life. They built permanent, or semipermanent, houses of logs in communities and spent at least part of the year in these houses. They began to use the Whiteman language among themselves and their children; they accepted Whiteman law that appeared to regulate society so well. Whitemen enjoyed liquor and consumed a lot of it. So did Indians. Whitemen gathered children together for periods of time during the year in order to give them instruction. Indians, at some personal sacrifice to the family economy, allowed their children to be gathered and instructed in Whiteman schools, which were provided especially for Indians by the churches. Many good Whitemen valued Indian women highly as wives, and Indian families willingly assented to such alliances.

Not all of this was a one-way process. Many early Whitemen moved as far toward the Indian way of life as did the Indians toward the Whitemen. Indian subsistence techniques away from the towns were—and still are—all but essential for survival. The economic survival of most Yukon residents of those early years required their subsisting for varying periods of the year away from the towns. In addition to Whiteman-Indian marriages, many partnerships were formed between Indians and Whitemen for varying periods of time, usually for trapping or for transporting supplies.

But as the growth of Whiteman population accelerated, the pervading sentiment of Whiteman society as a whole was that of unawareness of the Indians rather than anything else, and the new society's purposes tended to extend beyond the Indians' conceptual range. Indians were fine bush partners; they were inappropriate as store-keepers, as guests at tea parties, as bankers or mayors, or in a host of other roles the Whiteman brought with him to this new land.

Built into the Whiteman culture are internal conflicts; value conflicts which most Whitemen understand and can cope with, but which, to Indians, are gross inconsistencies that with time came to be viewed as evidences of moral degeneration. As awareness of these conflicts grew, reaction set in among the Indians, but set in too late to stem the tide of accumulated acculturation patterns.

TWENTIETH-CENTURY DEVELOPMENTS

The gold rush and the building of the Alaska Highway during the Second World War brought to the Yukon the full impact of modern, technological urbanization. These two massive events were of increasing importance to the Indians, but their participation in them was increasingly less important to Whitemen as the nature of the Yukon economy changed from direct demand for resources that the Indians could best supply to a more general resource exploitation utilizing machinery and skilled mechanical labor.

The gold rush, beginning in 1898, was over almost before the majority of Yukon residents were fully aware of it. The three-year flood of humanity which swept over every drainage represented more people and equipment than had ever been in the Yukon in all the preceding years (Berton 1958). It left behind piles of discarded artifacts; a large amount (in relation to usual income) of money spent as wages for Indian packers, guides, hunters, and housekeepers; a considerable genetic input; and a sprinkling of upper-middle-class permanent Whiteman residents to manage further exploitation of the mineral wealth. The real impact upon Yukon Indians was not money itself—most of the money left the territory—but an increased awareness of the importance of money as a symbol of status in Whiteman society. Increasing numbers of Indians concentrated around the settlements that remained after the gold rush. More and more Indians became dependent upon the market economy and upon wages earned during the summer to supplement their basic subsistence.

The Whiteman population of these settlements was a new and transient population without the missionary-trader interest in Indians. It comprised mostly colonial-minded traditionalists who came to the Territory for the sole purpose of exploiting its wealth. Unaccustomed to such rigorous living, they made every effort to transfer material comforts and social niceties from their homeland to the new country in which they lived only until such time as they could get out. The term "outside" became referent for all the good things available to them in more civilized areas, to which they aspired to return. By inference, the Yukon was substandard in all respects. From this population came an economic competition on the part of Whitemen which was beyond the comprehension of Indians, but which they felt keenly.

Between 1900 and 1940 a pattern stabilized whereby a spring influx of skilled and semiskilled immigrant Whitemen provided the primary labor pool. Indians also obtained jobs, but always at the bottom of the social and wage scale. Indians were the last to be hired as well as the first to be fired and were seldom accorded wages comparable to those of Whitemen. Being "uneducated" and "undependable," Indians were neither offered more skilled work nor trained for it. Since there was no dependability in wagework for Indians, the Yukon Indians' basic source for subsistence and money often remained the seasonal hunts and trapping (which, fortunately, left much free summer time); thus they became even more "undependable" in Whiteman terms. Even today, many Yukon Whitemen will tell you that you can ". . . never depend on an Indian to do a job. He'll take off to the hills after the first moose he sees!" The Indians soon became a marginal socioeconomic fringe of their adopted communities, dependent upon uncomprehended world fur-price fluctuations and unpredictable, occasional wage jobs. Inevitably, feelings of differences between exploiter and exploited widened the gaps between Indian and Whiteman and led to the development of prejudices and stereotypes among both.

When public schools began in the new towns, Indians were excluded and Indian schooling became a church function by default. Missionaries had originally expended most of their efforts toward Indian welfare, but it was from Whitemen that the churches derived their basic sanction and support and it was to Whitemen that the churches turned for "real development" as the economy of the Yukon prospered.

Priests and ministers committed more to a particular faith than to the Indian population came to the territory from southern Canada and from Europe, parishes were stabilized, and a typical set of "outside" church practices established.

Not that the churches abandoned Indians. Quite the contrary: the churches provided many essential community services—including schools—when neither the communities nor the Dominion government offered anything to the Indians. But the primary social identifications, and most social interactions, of church personnel were within the Whiteman group, a group that no longer shared common interests with Indians.

The second massive event was the building of the Alaska Highway during World War II. This had the dual effect of widening the gulf of misunderstanding between Indians and resident Whitemen and providing the Indians with new mechanisms for adaptation to the dominant society. Once again, as during the gold rush, an unbelievable horde of strangers descended overnight for a totally undreamed-of purpose. Once again material artifacts flooded into the country, men could work for good wages almost any time, and exciting things happened everywhere.

A significant difference between the gold rush and the highway construction was the amount of concomitant social interaction between the strangers and the Indians. The highway builders, intense as was their effort, were less single-mindedly seeking personal enrichment and were eager to devote more leisure time to informal interactions. These people, foreign to the Yukon, tended to treat Indians with the same consideration they gave to resident Whitemen; in some cases even more because it was from Indians that they got the best guide service, the best dog-team drivers, the best survival techniques. Moreover, they put Indians into trucks and jeeps and made drivers of them, paid them the same wages as Whitemen, and then danced and got drunk with them on off-duty hours. Some even married Indian girls and took them home, or settled permanently in the Territory. Thus ended the era of Indian subservience and mute acceptance of dependency as a not quite acceptable coinhabitant with Whitemen. This attitude has not been replaced with anything identifiable except a sullen determination to "secure rights," to insist upon recognition, and above all to reject total identification with the Whiteman if it means anything less than total acceptance of Indians as Indians.

Following the highway construction and the opening of the Canadian northland to regular travel, the Canadian Parliament passed the Indian Act, the first official affirmation of the existence of a set of reciprocal rights and obligations between Yukon Indians and the government. Many factors were responsible for the government policy change: a growing realization of the importance of the north country to Canada's economy and national defense, a world-wide consideration for the human rights of minority groups, an emerging Canadian welfare-state philosophy, and the collective conscience pangs of the non-Indian population of Canada.

That the Indian Act (Government of Canada 1952) is in some respects arbitrary, self-aborting, and overly paternalistic, is not so important as is the immediate and pervasive effect it has had upon Yukon Indian life. Government welfare provisions are extended to Indians, including family allowances as received by all other Canadian families; old-age social security payments; unemployment and disability insur-

A new highway town in the Yukon Territory. The panorama along the Alaska Highway—gas stations, a few stores, and housing merging into the bush—is the pattern.

ance; direct relief; aid to dependent children; and educational facilities equal to, or integrated with, Whiteman schools.

While legislation and attitude changes may well be the most lasting legacies of the Highway, the immediate changes came from mobility. Until the Highway, Indians moved by foot, by boat, or by dog team; even motors on boats had done little to change the principal routes or to extend by much the range of travel. Indians moved from lake to lake by way of rivers or creeks, with a minimum of overland travel, and they tended to be bound closely to the local trading store by credit relations that were never in their favor.

The Alaska Highway literally opened the door to the world, and Indians moved. They rapidly acquired automobiles and moved from town to town: a construction job here, a friend to visit there, some wood to be cut in another place, the big town to be visited for a goodtime, and always the hope that enough wage credit could be earned during the summer to qualify for unemployment insurance during the winter. Sullen resentment has not decreased as Indians experience over and over again the job discrimination that restricts employment opportunities and potential earnings, but at least a man is no longer stuck. He can always go "up the highway," an expression that has great meaning especially for adolescent Indians.

After the Highway opened, some towns completely disappeared as riverboat transportation became obsolete. In their places is a line of new towns along the highway, dominated by metropolitan Whitehorse where whole new patterns of ex-change of goods and services are generated by competition made possible by the Highway. Absolute dependence upon a single trader or trading company is gone. Supermarkets with weekly sales flourish in Whitehorse, and the old credit system is being broken. Hospital and health services provided by the government have result-ed in radical growth of the total Indian population. Even the most traditional activ-ities are affected by the highway. No longer is the spring beaver season a four-month period of major activity beginning in February with the setting of traps under the ice and continuing with regular runs until May. People now wait for the May thaw and travel by auto to a series of lakes where they quickly shoot the available beaver, skin them out, and transport them by car or trailer back to town. Beaver *trapping* has all but disappeared. Similar influences affect other hunting patterns, with most "hunting" time now being spent in planning logistics and arranging for transportation. Thus, even more leisure time is now available to the Indians since the basic job discrimination has not vanished; nearly all steady jobs and most sea-sonal employment are still held by immigrant Whiteman workers.

(During 1962–1963, the year of this study, a new vocational school was built in Whitehorse. It was expected that Indians would become students at this school. In constructing the school, Indians were not used to any appreciable extent, however, even though maintaining a labor supply was the single largest problem faced by the contractor who complained that he continually had ". . . one crew coming, one crew working and one crew going . . ." to and from Vancouver. The unemployment level among Indians remained about the same during the construction period.)

Today the Yukon Indian is culturally deprived, economically deprived, and living as a transitional migrant in his own homeland. He is extremely ambivalent in his attitudes, uncertain as to whether he should fight or capitulate—and even about what he *could* fight or to whom he could capitulate. Although identifiable persis-tences of attitude, behavior, language, and the individualistic aspects of native cul-ture are still present, the essential common characteristics of Yukon Indians today are poverty and a low level of participation in community affairs. What Oscar Lewis has referred to as the "sub-culture of poverty" (Lewis 1961)—"a set of transitory patterns by which a once-primitive population strives to make at least a peripheral adaptation to rapid urbanization by another society"—is more valid as a description of the present Yukon Indian population than any idealized traditional cultural base-line.

MATT MATHEWS' FAMILY: YUKON TERRITORY, 189- –1962

The following brief history of the Mathews family over four generations illus-trates general experiences that have been common to a majority of Yukon Indian families. It shows the relative meaninglessness of legalisms in identifying Indian and non-Indian. Although such terms tend to fragment families, the underlying kinship patterns persist and family unity is a function of these feelings rather than of legal identity.

Other commonalities typical of most Yukon families and represented in the

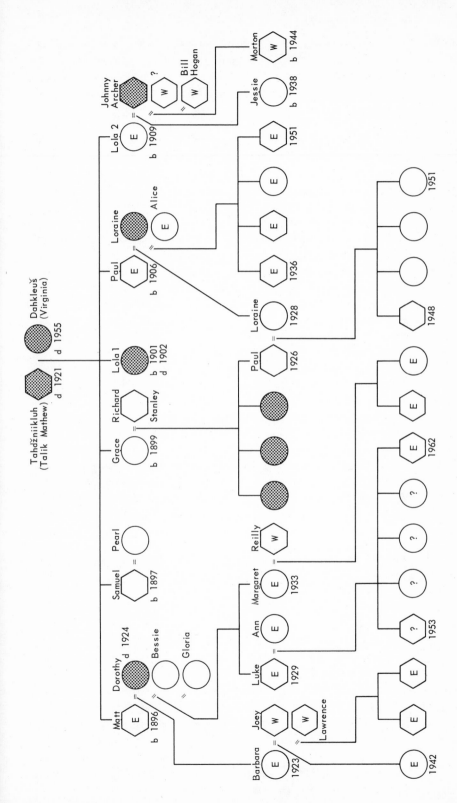

The Mathews Family, 1962: (E) indicates enfranchised members; (W) indicates Whiteman members; blank forms indicate members of the family who are "legally" Indian; hatched forms indicate the deceased.

Mathews family are: abandonment of Indian names; enfranchisement methods and results; preferred cross-cousin marriage, a matrilineal kinship system, with a moiety-like dichotomy of kin identity based upon the mother's identity as either a Wolf or a Crow (Raven). Most families have at least one member who has approached success in Whiteman terms but has fallen short of complete entry into Whiteman society. An elder male is usually acknowledged as "head of the family," although he most often maintains his own nuclear household; and an elder female (probably his sister or his mother's sister) bears the knowledge of family relationships and of the pool of available family names. Incest, aside from the parent-sibling relationship, is defined as a Wolf-Wolf or Crow-Crow relationship, and the elder female expert is consulted on all potential marriage relationships as well as on all names. Despite the government-imposed patrilineal system of family structure and naming, most families have managed to maintain their traditional structure (see diagram of the Mathews family, p. 13).

Also typical are the Mathews family's residence patterns, modes of subsistence, school experiences and memories of those experiences, attitudes toward school and Whitemen, and degrees of native language understanding and use—the last sharply differentiated by generation.

The account begins with Tahdžniikluh and Dahkleuš, mother and father respectively of two boys and a girl when the gold rush took place, and subsequently to have two more daughters and another son.

Today, knowledge about the antecedent families of Tahdžniikluh and Dahkleuš is very dim. She was Wolf and he was Crow. The descendents of one of her sisters are well known; a brother of Dahkleuš is known to have married but moved away, and his family is not known to the Mathews family. Tahdžniikluh had at least one brother and one sister, but they, too, have no place in the present family memory. Tahdžniikluh was not a young man in the 1890s and was about twenty years older than his wife. He was known as a good provider and a good friend. During the gold rush, he occasionally worked for Whitemen as a guide and packer, more often as an entrepreneur hunter who provided moose and caribou for sale to various camps. His basic life cycle was the traditional pattern of season migration. All his children were "born under a spruce tree," as they like to put it nowadays.

Tahdžniikluh became identified as Talik Mathew by Whitemen who could not pronounce his name. Talik was a good fish lake where Tahdžniikluh usually made his winter camp; Mathew resulted from the fact that four families camped at the lake and nearby Whitemen came to refer to them as Matthew, Mark, Luke, and John (all of which are still the family names today).

About the turn of the century, Talik Mathew's wife decided to accept baptism from an Anglican missionary. Talik Mathew himself was never baptised, but his wife became Virginia and his eldest son was baptised as "Mathew, son of Talik Mathew and Virginia Mathew." Other children were similarly baptised Samuel, Grace, Lola and Paul. Lola died in infancy, and the sixth child of Tahdžniikluh and Dahkleuš was also named Lola. This was consistent with their traditional practice in cases of infant death followed by the birth of a child of the same sex. All the children also had Indian names given at appropriate times with appropriate ceremony, but these names were not told to church authorities for recording, nor were they used for everyday identification within the family.

Until the oldest son was about ten years old, the family remained together and their life pattern was completely traditional with the father earning supplementary cash income in fairly consistent, but relatively insignificant (from a subsistence standpoint) amounts. By that time the Mopass school had become firmly established and the minister urged parents to send their children to the school. The boy Mathew was sent to school in his tenth year. At school he was called Matt Mathews, his name today. Matt already knew some English, learned mainly from his father and friends, but English had not been used much in his home. His mother, Virginia, never did really command the language although she lived until 1955.

Until he went to school, Matt's life experience had been a gradually expanding awareness of his physical environment: he helped around the house and derived his greatest pleasure from being allowed to help his father in hunting, trapping, and general subsistence tasks. He knew Whitemen by sight, but had little direct contact with them. His clothing and food were much the same as what his father had known as a child.

Matt spent four years at Mopass School; he remembers doing especially well in arithmetic and learning how to read and write, but he also remembers how he hated the restrictive routine. When he was fifteen, he decided that he had to help his family and, with his father's encouragement, left school to ". . . begin to learn how a man *should* make his living." His father taught him to trap and to hunt and fish, and in the next two years the two of them established a relatively thriving business of providing meat for the railroad, the school, and occasional miners. They came to depend on that money and money from trapping as their principal source of subsistence. More and more food purchased in stores entered the family diet. From his new status as family supporter, Matt encouraged his siblings to become educated by going to the mission school. His father was growing old and his mother was frequently ill. Besides being a generally approved course of action, having the children away at school during the winters relieved some of the burden of their care. Samuel, Grace, and Paul spent six years at the mission school. Samuel did especially well and was later employed as a junior bookkeeper at the railroad office. The family was very proud of him, although Mathew confesses that ". . . .I never really understood Sam; why he was willing to give up everything and work in that office. But he was always a deep one; always thinking."

By the time young Paul was established in the school, Matt had experienced the elation of making a quick pile of money as guide for a Whiteman hunter, had invested his money in a horse and a boat for more such trips, and had secured his parent's permission to marry Dorothy, a daughter of one of the families that had lived near the Mathews for many years during wintertime. Dorothy had also been in school with Matt. His first child, a daughter, was born in 1923, and Matt felt himself surging forward in life. Married and with a family begun, he had money, ability, recognition as a person of worth from both Whitemen and Indians, and a desire to become an even bigger man in the community.

Grace was a demure, conventional child. She progressed in school quite well, seldom had troubles, and learned housekeeping tasks especially well along with reading and writing. She internalized the religious dogma of the Anglican church and remained a staunch Women's Auxiliary member throughout her life. When Grace was sixteen, her mother's health became really poor and she left school to care for the family house. The winter camp site had been near the route of the railroad, and Matt and his father had gradually enlarged and made permanent the old winter home building. Meanwhile Matt had built another log house for himself nearby. The settlement that sprang up along the railroad was a scant half mile away and the Mathews found themselves part of a town community.

Two years later Grace was married to Richard Stanley, a friend of her older brother and also a hunter and trapper of considerable renown. Richard's father and Grace's father were also old friends, but unrelated. Richard's mother and Grace's mother had some relatives in common, but the relationships were not well defined or (today) exactly remembered except that Richard is, of course, a Crow. Richard and Grace lived with her father and mother until the flu epidemic of 1921 when Talik Mathew died. Matt and Richard then cooperated in building a new house nearer to Matt's place. This was known as "Virginia's house," but Richard and Grace maintained the house and still live there. The old place was abandoned and today is little more than a barely visible home site.

Dorothy never fully recovered from childbirth and, after about a year of prolonged illness, she died. Grace was left with the task of maintaining both homes until Matt remarried. Richard Stanley never went to school. After his marriage, he began to work more and more often as a railroad section hand during the summers and, as Matt developed a fur-fox farm and a boat rental business, Richard worked with him to the extent that Richard's personal hunting and trapping activities dwindled to little more than an occasional trip to provide meat for the family. Both men were essentially dependent on cash income, although they still ate much wild meat and fish and still made extensive use of animal skins for shoes and winter clothing.

Paul, the youngest son of Talik Mathew, continued in residential mission school until he was almost seventeen. Although he did not particularly care for most aspects of the life, he became the school printer and he dearly loved that job. A small hand press had been obtained for publication of a church newsletter, and Paul was the typesetter. In this capacity he learned to read well and probably read much more than most children. The skill was also responsible for relieving him of some of the routine tasks of school maintenance which were burdensome to most children. A final attraction of the school was the presence of his second-wife-to-be, Alice, with whom he was already enamored.

When Paul left school, it was to take a job in the city (50 miles away) as a typesetter at the newspaper shop where he worked at piecework rates. He was good, and this work provided him with steady income for several years during which he maintained a rented residence in town. Occasionally he returned to fish or hunt with Matt, but he gave primary attention to his printing job. In the flush of blossoming maturity and wealth, he was married to Loraine, a women whom his mother had long before selected as being his appropriate wife. They had a daughter, also named Loraine. Alice, after finishing school and being needed at home, had returned to live unmarried with her family for the next few years.

Lola, the baby of the family, was pampered and petted by others in the family, especially after her father's death. She attended the residential mission school for eight years, encouraged by her family, who relieved her of any necessity to have family work obligations and who believed that she would become the "lady of the family." When she married Johnny Archer, the son of a former Royal Canadian Mounted Policeman who, even before the gold rush, had quit the force and taken both an Indian wife and the Indian way of life, the Mathews family rejoiced at the perfect marriage. Lola had liked school, had made very good marks, and had even aspired for a time to become a teacher. However, marriage changed that. Johnny's family was not poor, and she looked forward perhaps to moving to a larger town or even outside someday. Their daughter, Jessie, was born in 1938.

Meanwhile Matt married again. He needed a wife to care for his house and daughter. Bessie was from a family long known to his family. Even before Lola was married, Matt and Bessie had two more children. Grace and Richard also had children, but had very bad luck. All their children died until their son Paul (who shared his uncle's Indian name as well as his Christian name) at last lived, and then they had no more.

To this point—roughly, the decade of the 1930s—life for the children of Tahdž-niikluh and Dahkleuš had its ups and downs, but in general had been good. It was much changed from their own childhood. All of them spoke English almost all of the time except to their mother and a few others of the old ones. Particularly they spoke English to their children because they wanted their children to be comfortable with the language. Aside from this, in their daily lives so much was new and different with no linguistic referent, or had such a very cumbersome form in the native language, that English was simply easier to use. All of them had Indian names and knew the Indian names of their birth, but there was seldom much opportunity for lengthy exchanges about old families or friends or customs. Only Grace, through her long years of caring for Virginia, really became knowledgeable and fluent in the family genealogy. The world depression had tumbled fur prices, and jobs were minimal but still available. Hunting and fishing were always good, and some men still came from the "outside" who could afford these pleasures at the regular prices. Matt had to rent only a few boats during the year to break even and in most years he continued to make a tidy profit. There was a slight tightening of income sources among others, but nothing to be overly worried about. A sort of family euphoria prevailed.

But this was a peak experience for the family as a whole and for the individuals within it. One by one the barriers became perceived, the tragedies struck, shattering events compounded upon one another, and the downgrade began.

With Matt, it began with Bessie's increasing unhappiness about being left alone while he was off fishing or trying to drum up business. She began seeking friendships at the local bar and eventually moved into the city world of bright lights, staying away from home for longer and longer periods of time until Matt became disgusted and obtained a divorce. Bessie completely disappeared after a few more years and after having several more children by a varied set of sires.

Matt refused to marry again for a long time, but he did take into his house Gloria and her teen-age daughter. They were old friends of the family and at the time were refugees from a Whiteman husband and father much further north who had been extremely cruel to them. Gloria was in the process of getting her divorce.

Matt had been experiencing increasing frustration in his dealings with sportsmen when he could not accompany them into bars. He chafed at the Indian discrimination. He also was quite unhappy with some of the residential school personnel and withdrew his children from the school. He sought and obtained enfranchisement, an act that made his children and wife also legally non-Indian. The children were put into city schools and came home only on weekends and during summers. Gloria was "Mom" to them, and for a time it seemed as if they were living a typical Whiteman middle-class pattern common to families who were remote from schools.

But then, all too soon, Matt's daughter Barbara had a daughter of her own and no husband. While in the tenth grade she had become increasingly unhappy at the social barriers in the town society and decided to have some "fun out of life." Gradually she had dropped out of school and one night while she was drunk, became pregnant. Her daughter's father was a Whiteman whom she never saw again. Matt brought the two other children, Luke and Margaret, home to live and to attend the little local public school.

Paul lost his job as a typesetter when Linotype machines were introduced. For a year or so afterward, he worked occasionally on jobs requiring handset type, but then he was out completely. In his few attempts at learning, he just could not master the Linotype machine. Loraine died from pneumonia contracted during an all-night drinking bout in midwinter; and Paul found himself alone in town with a daughter, no wife, and no job. He returned to the home settlement, married Alice, and began to work on the railroad during summers. During the World War II years he worked briefly as a guide and tractor operator, but he never again attempted to enter the city labor market. He and Alice had several children, all of whom became enfranchised when Paul followed the lead of Matt and enfranchised himself. Perhaps one of the first technologically unemployed persons in the Yukon Territory, Paul never fully recovered from the shock of finding that his skill as a typesetter was no longer needed. After the war he drifted into a pattern of occasional jobs with the railroad and almost complete dependence upon Matt for whom he worked almost regularly as caretaker, repairman, and occasional fishing guide when business was very good.

Paul says that, to this day, he cannot tell why he was so foolish as to get enfranchised. "What did it do for me? I can buy liquor and I can pay taxes and who needs *them?*" In 1962 he was a friendly but sodden alcoholic whose wife and brother supported him. He was very favorably disposed toward schools and wanted all his children to attend school. "Let 'em get all the education they can; then let 'em get to hell out of this country where there's nothing but prejudice!"

Samuel never married as a young man. All these years he had been a regular employee at the railroad office. He had had a few pay raises as the general economic level rose, but no promotions. When the Alaska Highway construction began, he was still junior bookkeeper although several Whitemen younger than he had held the senior position in his office during that time. Sam lived alone in a small cabin, often visiting his family and frequently contributing money for family affairs, but doing most of his own housework, cooking, and so on. He surprised everybody by quitting the railroad and taking a job with a highway contractor where he stayed until the job was completed. He then moved into the city and got a job as timekeeper with the regular highway maintenance force. He married an Indian girl considerably younger than he was, and for nearly ten years they lived in the city. They have no children, and in 1955 he quit his city job and moved with his wife to a remote site at the far end of the lake where Matt lives, perhaps 3 miles from his brother. Samuel has lost his railroad seniority, works only very occasionally at odd jobs around town for a few dollars, gets a little help from Matt, and is looking forward to drawing an old-age pension. "Why did I move out of town? Well, I guess I'd just as soon starve as live that kind of life any more. I had good money and lots of friends; in fact, the two go together. The more money I had, the more friends I had. All of them expecting me to buy liquor and food for them. . . . No, I never got franchised but nobody has ever questioned me about buying liquor. I guess they just all figure that I was franchised long ago. . . . Well, we lived in town nearly ten years and I had good work. Lots of times we had parties at my house and most of the time somebody else besides us was living with us. But all this time we were never invited to any Whiteman's house. Sure, they came to my house. I was running a goddam boarding house there and I couldn't tell those people to get out. So we got out. That's all. Out here I like it and I don't need nobody."

Lola's husband, Johnny, went to war when the draft took him. When the United States Army came to town to guard and work on the railroad, Lola went to work as a waitress in a local café. She was pretty and popular and soon pregnant with Morton. At first she was a little sad that this child would not be Johnny's, but she was not ashamed. She felt that Johnny would understand. Before she could get around to telling him, however, a local rival for Johnny's affections wrote several poison pen letters to Johnny about his wife's behavior. When he found that his wife was really pregnant by another man, he never returned. After the war he immediately filed for divorce and then spent the next fifteen years drifting from town to town and from job to job; finally he drowned one night when he fell into the river while drunk.

Lola and her son lived with Matt for several years. Later Matt sent them to the city to live so Jessie could go to school but have her mother there to watch over her. Lola worked as a waitress or chambermaid for a while and gradually "took up with" Bill Hogan. Eventually she married him. Her daughter retained Johnny's last name, but to her son she gave Matt's name. Lola automatically became enfranchised when she finally married Bill Hogan, but Jessie was over twenty-one by that time and free to choose for herself. She chose to remain Indian. Morton, however, admittedly had a non-Indian father and is legally forbidden Indian status.

Paul, son of Grace and Richard, also went to war. When he returned, still unmarried, he immediately gratified the dream of his mother and others in the family by marrying his mother's brother's first daughter, Loraine, with whom he had four children in quick succession. Paul and Loraine had both attended the mission residential school. Paul hated it and was grateful to the war for having rescued him from further school. He liked the outdoors and hunting and had no intention of becoming a wage slave as he felt his father had. He constantly urged his father to give up the railroad work and return to trapping and hunting with him, but Richard was feeling older and was satisfied with his security of summer work and winter unemployment insurance.

Loraine, just out of school when married, had ideas other than being a trapper's wife. She wanted to go to the city and did so more and more frequently, finally obtaining a job there after her fourth child was born. Paul and Loraine had been quite atypical in having a child each year for four years. At least a two-year interval was expected. This was indicative of the growing tension between them, interpreted by Loraine as a lack of consideration for her and a desire to "trap" her and by Paul as a growing coolness and rejection of him because he ". . . wasn't good enough for her." So their marriage was lost before it matured. Lola left the children in Grace's care until they were old enough to be placed in the residential school. Paul hunted and trapped and took odd jobs, but mostly became drunk oftener and oftener. He has one of the most unique arrest records in the Yukon, where few Indians do not have some record of arrests. Paul's was lengthy and imaginative: not just simple intoxication and never for serious offenses or offenses while sober. He was known to be a strong worker and a "good guy" while sober, but all too few employers were finding it worthwhile to wait for him him to become sober and he was getting less and less work in the 1960s. At that time Loraine had steady housekeeping work and had long ago said she would never return.

After the war Matt married Gloria and thus automatically enfranchised her. Barbara took care of her own enfranchisement. She kept out of further difficulty, worked as a waitress for a while, and then married a steady young Whiteman from the south where she moved with her daughter and husband and still lives. Gloria did not like being married to Matt and did not like the idea of being enfranchised. Matt now thinks she married him only to get a claim on his money for she soon divorced him, was awarded a property settlement, and immediately married another Indian man and regained Indian status.

For all the years Gloria had been with Matt, she had been the person called "Mom" by Luke and Margaret. At the time of the divorce, eighteen-year-old Luke was particularly confused. He admired his father tremendously and aspired to be a good fishing and hunting guide himself, but he disliked his father's rejection of Indin status. Then the divorce and apparent rejection by his "mother" disturbed him even more. He had been a mediocre student at school, getting to the ninth grade before quitting altogether in 1948. He saw no reason to continue if he was going to be an outdoorsman. He also saw no difference in people's attitudes toward him after he had been enfranchised along with his father. He was still looked on as an Indian and he spent the next few years almost defiantly asserting himself as the possessor of all the bad attributes which the traditionalist Whiteman considered town Indians to have. Luke took an Indian wife, but did not marry her. They had four children before he finally consented to become legally married. (His first four children are thus technically of legal Indian status, having been born of an unmarried Indian woman.) Meanwhile, Luke drank almost continually except when he was working. He became one of the best fishing guides in the Territory by the time he was twenty-one—and one of the most undependable. He barely tolerated Whiteman sportsmen from outside; he abused them while on trips and had even abandoned them when they turned out to be "poor sports." He stole cars and wrecked them. He disappeared and reappeared broke and needing a drink. He loved his woman—and frequently beat her up. Luke's family, mostly his father, took care of his children's basic needs beyond what government assistance to the unmarried mother provided. In 1962, when he finally married, he took his family to live in a cabin 20 miles up an old mining road from Matt's home, on a trapping claim that his father helped him to obtain. He was pleased with the arrangement, asserting proudly, "By God, me and my kids are going to live like Indians *should* live!" At official levels, however, there was considerable doubt that he or his children could ever regain Indian status.

All of the Mathews family at that generational level—Barbara, Luke, Margaret, Paul, Loraine, Bessie, and Morton—speak English fluently and do not speak their native language at all except a few greeting words to elders of their grandfather's generation. All of them have Indian names, but never use them. Morton and Luke were reluctant even to speak their Indian names, at least to the Whiteman inquirer. When they were asked about names, they suggested that Grace should be asked. "She knows all them things," they said.

All of the generation had gone to school longer than had their parents, but only Jessie finished high school. Jessie, retaining her Indian status and urged on by Matt and the others, had gone through specialized vocational training beyond high school and was employed full-time in 1962, one of the five Indians in the entire Territory who had education beyond high school at that time. She had liked school, although she spoke of, ". . . working hard only because mother and uncle wanted me to . . ." and of bitter social experiences that made her cry at times. All the others had liked school classes up to a point, but had ". . . got fed up with . . ." the attitudes of teachers or students or both, and all the other Mathews said they had quit school.

Of the entire family, the only members who remain legal Indians in the government definition are Richard and Grace, their son, Paul, his wife and children, plus Jessie and possibly Luke's first four children (about whom final determination had not yet been made). Yet the family remains an entity in the sense that any member could enter any other member's house with expectation of hospitality beyond that shown to nonfamily and with the expectation of respect or support behavior from the others in accordance with traditional attitudes toward the relationship involved. Matt's children call him "Dad." All other members of that generation call him "Uncle." The next generation all call him "Grandfather." Everyone in the family refers to him as "the boss of this family."

All of the children of the family who are currently of school age are in public schools with the exception of Paul and Loraine's offspring. The latter are in the residential school by direction of the Indian Affairs Branch, which adjudge them to be children of a broken home despite the extensive family that would be willing to care for the children. Each marriage group has constituted a separate household. At various times help has been given and major tasks shared, but aside from such assistance, there have been no combinations of married peers for the purpose of establishing permanent residence and the children have been raised in a home where mother and father—or at least one of those—are recognized as the head of the household.

The present children of the family were all born in hospitals. They know little of their Indian heritage except the single name—which some have forgotten until reminded—and their Wolf or Crow identification, which all know. A few "right" ways to do certain discrete tasks or to behave in certain social situations may have had greater significance than simple behavior directives in past times; now they are just directives, however. There are no ceremonial events, no adult societies, no established body of regulatory concepts other than those of the Whiteman. These children wear the same kinds of clothing as non-Indian children; occasionally they have finer moccasins, usually their other clothing is not so fine. Until at least sixth grade and adolescence there is little social distinction among Indian and non-Indian children themselves.

Social contacts between Indian and Whiteman adults are limited, however. Only one of the households described here had a Whiteman next door neighbor; all the others lived in areas where only other Indian families reside. The one with the Whiteman neighbor has a cordial, but rather distant relationship with that neighbor. Occasionally they share tools or outdoor conversations, but seldom enter each other's houses except for specified, limited purposes such as giving a message or asking for information about some event.

However, no overt evidence of discrimination was observed either in face-to-face conversations with Indians or in conversations between Whiteman parents and their children. In fact, the most derogatory references to Indians that were heard in this town came from mothers who were themselves of Indian descent when they forbade their children to play with "those dirty Indian kids" across the river. These same women, in other contexts, would speak with pride of their Indian family. The quality of being Indian or possessing Indian attributes in the Yukon is indeed elusive.

FAMILIES OF RESIDENTIAL SCHOOL CHILDREN

The upper class (fourth grade) at Mopass Residential School in 1962 contained children from twenty-two families in addition to the Mathews-related Stanley children. Through extended interviews, through the knowledge a teacher acquires of students during a school year, and through further observations, the following summary of family structures and relationships as perceived by the children was obtained. All these children met the government definitions of Indian and thus were permitted or required to live at the school with full subsistence provided for the ten months of the school year.

Every family has relatives known to the children, but every family constitutes a separate household with a father or mother or both as head of the house, which is a separate dwelling. Two thirds of the children identified at least one enfranchised member in their known kin group; in several cases, family age-mates (cousins) are enfranchised and thus non-Indian, although this makes no apparent difference in relationships.

Although they all know some relatives by name, less than half the children could name two grandparents and these could do so only when the grandparents were still living. All the children have Whiteman names derived from their parents. All of them also have Indian names and a Wolf or Crow identification derived from their mothers. Exactly half the children insisted that they did not have "Indian" names when they were first questioned. At least one seemed genuinely surprised to discover that he does indeed have such a name. In spite of this, all but two correctly identified themselves as Wolf or Crow when first asked.

Each child belongs to a government-designated "band," which has a name and number. In addition, each child has a personal identification number. The bands were arbitrarily established when the Indian Act was passed and bear no relation to any identity designation known to Indians, being mostly Whiteman place names. Indians who happened to be living there at the time of designation were declared members of that band. Children of the school know their band name when it corresponds with the place name that is their referent for home; otherwise they do not know it. None of the children knew anything about numbers, band or personal. Yet for official purposes, now and all through their lives as Indians, the band names and numbers will be essential identification attributes for them.

The families tend to be large in comparison with Whiteman families; they range from two to ten children and average over six children per family. The regularity with which children are born at two- to three-year intervals in most families supports other accounts heard of a long post partum taboo against sexual relations, which reportedly was rigidly adhered to in the traditional society. Women say that they enjoy having children and like to have babies around the house. No family among those represented at school has only one child, even though some of the mothers have not married legally and even more of them were not married at their first child's birth.

Only five of the twenty-two families have no knowledge of some non-Indian admixture to the family line within the past two generations; yet if any of these had resulted in a legal marriage, the individual would by definition not be Indian today. Marriage is not particularly valued as an institution; when convenient, it is a natural event. Often, when legal marriage means loss of Indian status or loss of family-welfare support money, it is dispensed with. (An unmarried mother with three or four children is an attractive economic partner for a male who wishes to have a home life without too great a burden of support involved.)

Residence patterns of the families reflect the high mobility of Yukon Indians and their lack of attachment to a house as "home." Invariably, Indian people in the Yukon use the verb "to stay" when referring to residence in a building. "To live" has reference to a broader existence in a region, expansive and beyond any bounds of walls. One "stays" at a house or building with the implication that one is willing or expecting to move at any time. Only three of the twenty-two children were from the same residences in which their parents were living when the child was born, and twelve of the families no longer live in the same band region as the parents' parents had lived.

Nearly all the parents have been to school and all speak English to their children and with each other. None has gone beyond grade eight, and few that far. School attendance has no apparent relationship to employment. About half the men in the families still rely upon some form of traditional skills for the major portion of their income—trapping, hunting, or guiding are the most general. These men, rather than the ones whose major dependence is on wages, are more likely to have a marketable skill enabling them to obtain occasional employment above common labor. The most regularly employed parents are the few women who work as waitresses or chambermaids. No male parent has a full-time job; at the same time, no male parent earns all of his annual income from traditional self-employment.

For children, life within their parents' houses is mostly functional. Except for occasional visits by adults who sit around the kitchen table, the house is for eating, sleeping, storing and changing clothing, and very little else. Children do not have rooms to themselves alone; the houses tend to be minimal: two or three rooms of log or wood-frame construction with plank floors covered by linoleum, scatter rugs, or hides. The interiors are usually clean and order prevails, but it is a scattered sort of order in which little is hidden from sight. Beds, couches, or other sleeping areas are in every room except the kitchen. Clothing is hung on wall pegs or stored in boxes and chests around the room and under beds. Walls are usually papered and decorated further with photographs, magazine pictures, and religious pictures or artifacts. Indoor plumbing, if it exists at all, is limited to a single cold-water pipe at a sink. Kerosene or gas lanterns usually provide light, and potbellied or barrel stoves supplement the heat generated by the kitchen range. Usually both stove and range are wood-burning. Houses are often owned by the occupants or someone in the family, but the land is probably Crown land and the residents are squatters. (Squatters' rights are recognized in many parts of the Yukon, for both Indians and non-Indians.) Paint is seldom wasted on house exteriors, by many non-Indians as well as by Indians, and it is an unusual house that does not appear weather-beaten and somewhat dilapidated from the outside.

Even Indian children who live at home have few opportunities to participate with adults in subsistence or household tasks. Household chores are confined to bringing in wood and water and preparing or cleaning up after meals. As often as not these are done by the woman of the house. Children spend most of their days outside playing or roaming around town where they know almost everybody and everything that is going on.

When it is cold, children enter stores or other public buildings to stand quietly getting warm and watching adults. Most towns have one or more barrooms or taverns, and these are the scene of most adult socializing. Children are not permitted *in* the bars, but are often around outside or in adjacent dining rooms watching or waiting for their parents.

Although Indian parents become annoyed at children and speak sharply to them when they feel it necessary, they do not seem to become so angry as to have to strike their children. Baby hands are held away from stoves or matches or danger—occasionally with a spat or rapid slapping together of hands as a restraint—but physical punishment *after* the fact is seldom observed. A few children say they remember being "spanked" by their parents, but inquiry usually reveals that this has been more on the order of being slapped in the rear or on the hand during some moment of stress. None of the children could recount an incident of being turned over a knee with the common Whiteman, "This hurts me more than it does you," sequence of events. (Until they reach residential school, that is; for most Indian children, school provides their first experience with adults who deliberately inflict physical punishment upon children.)

Children frequently listen closely to adult conversations, but are seldom included. These conversations, mostly in English, seldom seem modified by the children's presence. Talk is usually about work, personal experiences, or local gossip. Stories of past time are mostly life experiences of the speakers, dealing with hunting trips or visitors, often having accounts of liquor-drinking bouts as climactic events. Beer or other liquor is usually being consumed as well as talked about. Whatever type of alcoholic beverage is available is completely consumed in the course of a visit.

One of the old ways of doing things: these miniature houses built over individual graves are one of the variable burial practices of the Yukon Indians today. Such houses are made of modern materials and are often better painted and tended than the survivors' houses.

(Rarely these days but—from stories heard—more frequently in the not so distant past, home brew made from almost anything was the most common beverage used. Since there are no bottling works in the Yukon, the wide use of commercial bottled beverages is another indication of the general rise in the economy resulting from the new highway.) Both immediate observation and verbal verification of past experiences leads any observer (especially children) to the conclusion that "fun" and pleasant social gatherings automatically involve consumption of the liquor available, preferably with the consumer becoming drunk.

Much singing takes place during such casual visits. The songs are mostly church hymns or American westerns. A few Indian songs are known by the older people, but these are never sung unless as a special favor upon request and then only by the person to whom the song "belongs," not by the group in the manner that all join in with "Rock of Ages." Several times after Indian adults had sung such songs, they were observed to direct questions to the children present, as if belatedly realizing that the children didn't know the song. "How you like that one, hey? You know what it say?" The children never did know, laughed in embarrassment when urged to try to sing, and struggled to escape. Older people said that their grandparents had told them many things in the course of routine living tasks when they were young, but generally agreed that they themselves had not talked as much to their own children. "Kids nowadays never get a chance to hear the old things. You know, a lot of them things is pretty hard to say in English." When pressed as to what kinds of "things," their answers tended to be vague. "Well, just *lots*a things. How people oughta act with each other and things you gotta do for your family and like that. I guess we *know* them things but we don't know no words to say. . . ."

The general poverty of Indian families seems not so much a lack of money as a lack of acquisitive concepts about money. Money always seems to be available from somewhere when needed. The average income per family per year would, indeed, seem at a poverty level in comparison with non-Indian incomes, but the proportion of expenditures for nonfood items would be much more divergent. Accumulation of property or artifacts for security is not so important to Indians as it is to Whitemen. In the old days, land and family were security enough and both are still there with, out expenditure of material wealth. To the extent that these facts no longer provide security, the government has taken over a large part of this function. Money tends to be an instrument for immediate gratification of wants, rather than a form of potential capital to be invested as an income-producing extension of one's work. If the money can be obtained, today's needs—shoes, a gun, a car, a beer—should be bought; there is no reason for waiting to have it later. Moreover, there is a great tendency to get "the best," regardless of comparable prices or quality. This attitude is pragmatic and present-oriented: one may never have anything like the purchased object again; therefore it should serve its purpose well and, since its selection will reflect one's judgment to others, the reflection should be as bright as possible. Credit for major purchases, long-term loans involving regular payments, or bank accounts of any sort are not a part of the usual Indian economic life in the Yukon.

Another topic of conversation often heard when Indian adults get together is that of enfranchisement. Those who have taken the step and have "lost" their Indian status are usually sorry and express this regret. Those of the elders who have resisted enfranchisement often chuckle in self-congratulation at having been astute enough to perceive the outcomes of enfranchisement. Before "integration" became the popular government policy word among Indian Affairs Branch officials, "assimilation" had been their key concept. For several years after the war agency superintendents had engaged in extensive proselyting efforts to get people to accept enfranchisement. There is now a very definite impression among Indians that, at one time, a superintendent's effectiveness was measured by the number of "Canadian citizens" he was able to produce from among the Indians in his agency.

The Indians and former Indians all agree that the only real change enfranchisement has brought is to add bothersome details about licensing for hunting and fishing and payment of taxes (from which Indians are exempt). Around election times various candidates come a-wooing all who can vote, but the ex-Indians seldom see or hear of these people after elections and perceive little results from having voted. More important, no new jobs or job opportunities have suddenly appeared for enfranchised adults. Opportunities for jobs and housing are, if anything, worse for them because the government does not help "citizens" as it does Indians.

Worse than the loss of government benefits, the older men agree, is the attitude of their young adult children who harbor deep resentment against the parents who "tossed away" their heritage without giving the children a chance to have a say in the matter. This irrevocable action, the elders are sure, is responsible for much of the trouble among the younger people. Of course, those who have retained Indian status absorb such conversations thoroughly and are reaffirmed in their determination never to allow such a thing to happen to *them*.

The home environment of today's Indian school children—generally, the fourth generation of this acculturation sequence—provides them with basic security and identity while at the same time it instills in them a basic insecurity and the realization that their identity is tentative, without firm roots. Physical subsistence needs are met, but Indian children quickly perceive unflattering differences between their own physical environment and that of Whitemen's children, and differences between the social status of non-Indian parents and their own parents in the Whiteman's world. In their families they hear tales of discrimination, of defeated aspirations, of misunderstandings that could not be explained. They learn to name themselves and their family members, and only later do they learn that these names are Whiteman's names and that they *might* have had another identity in another time. (Sometimes the Whiteman's name itself becomes a source of embarrassment with which the child must learn to cope: Joe Washpan or Tommy Scurvey may go to school the first time feeling some pride in his family identity, only to become the butt of hurtful jibes about his name, which sounds odd to the Whiteman's children.)

Despite all the perceptions of differences, his own family remains highly important to the child. Aside from names, his identity as a person loved and belonging remains in his family. His kinfolk are true security identifications, whether he has the ability to be explicit about them or not. So, from the child's earliest perceptions, his identity is reinforced as Indian opposed to Whiteman; Indian opposed to Canadian or any other nationality; and Indian as the source of real identity affirmation, no matter how tenuous the threads that bind an Indian to his heritage.

When residential school children were asked, "Who are Canadians?" they never included Indians. When they were shown pictures of Yukon residents and asked to identify people, they consistently differentiated between Canadians and Indians. On the other hand, when examining pictures of various Amerind groups, including the Navajo, Sioux, and Caribs, the children readily identified all of them as Indians and expressed surprise that there was any nationality differentiation among the groups.

Yukon Indians and their families have been artificially segmented by Whiteman influences. Both legislative definitions and religious identifications create identity terms that subdivide Indians in ways that serve no real social function. In spite of this, all people of Indian heritage appear to share a basic perception of mankind which makes primary differentiation between Indians as the "we" group and Whiteman as the "other" group. This perception persists even when the traditional culture has all but vanished. Those elements that linger seem to be a reactive defense mechanism for coping with the powerful, but generally apathetic Whiteman society rather than a deliberate or functional persistence of cultural traits as valued entities in themselves.

THE YUKON INDIAN AGENCY

When, after several generations of disregard, the Canadian government became actively interested in the Yukon Indians, it did so with good intentions but illfitting mechanisms. A bureaucracy and legal machinery that had operated only moderately well with "treaty Indians" elsewhere was extended to the Yukon where the unique Indian population was molded and fitted into prescribed administrative units. With practically no Indian participation or representation and usually with even less Indian understanding of the purposes behind government policies, the result has been a compounded confusion of misunderstandings.

To Yukon Indians, the agency and its superintendent *are* the government. From the central agency office in Whitehorse, Yukon Territory, the agency superintendent, two assistants, a vocational placement officer, and two clerks administer the affairs of fifteen "bands" of Indians located between the Arctic Circle to the north, the Alaska boundary on the west, and arbitrary lines to the east and south which do *not* coincide with the Dominion governmental unit known as the Yukon Territory (see frontispiece). The duties of the agency staff, stemming from the Indian Act legislation, are specified in great detail by an administrative handbook approximately four inches thick and bound in such a manner that replacement pages can be easily be inserted as directives come from the Ottawa headquarters. Top priority tasks include identification of Indians by established legal criteria and maintenance of up-to-date vital statistics that, in turn, form the basis for agency authorization of payments of monies from various sources for various purposes contributing to Indian welfare. The agency assists in health and other family emergencies; directs the education of all Indian children under sixteen years and as many over that age as are considered qualified and willing to attend school; and devotes other time as available to various schemes for community improvement, economic development, capital outlays, and "evaluation of progress."

The Yukon Indian Agency is the operational unit of the Indian Affairs Branch, a division of the Canadian Department of Citizenship and Immigration, both having headquarters in Ottawa, Ontario. In Vancouver, British Columbia, a Western Regional Headquarters is responsible for the administration of twenty Indian agencies, of which the Yukon is one. All personnel of the Indian Affairs Branch are civil service employees. Appointments and promotions are nearly always a matter of competitive examination and seniority. Agency superintendents traditionally began as junior clerks and work their way up. In some Canadian Indian agencies, Indians have been employed; occasionally they reach the status of senior administrator. This has not yet happened in the Yukon agency.

In 1962 the Whitehorse office was woefully undermanned and would still have been undermanned, even if the Whitehorse staff's duties had been limited to the few top priority tasks among the Indian population of nearly 3000—a population that is scattered over thousands of square miles and is constantly shifting. In such a case, it is almost inevitable that personnel should tend to seek refuge in office procedures to the exclusion of fieldwork. To add to the frustration of their trying to maintain some sort of contact with the remote population for whom they are responsible, agency personnel seem to undergo continual demands from higher authorities that "more attention be given to office procedures," along with demands for "more field contacts."

An unfortunate efficiency in the original establishment of "bands" and equally unfortunate in a basic census taken during the late 1940s is illustrative of the compounding of errors that makes administration of the Yukon Indian Agency so difficult. The concept of "band," which in some parts of Canada represents a corporate entity of Indians that becomes an effective administrative channel, is totally foreign to the Yukon Indians. Ottawa established the bands in order to identify all legal Indians and to divide them into named units. A thorough census was taken; lines were drawn on a map in Whitehorse; and, on a given date, all Indians residing within the areas represented by the lines were declared members of the bands. During the census, names were not cross-checked and families were not identified in their matrilineal structure. "Chiefs" and "councils" were also appointed (or, preferably, elected when enough band members could be collected to hold an election) by government order—again, Ottawa disregarded the lack of any antecedent for such roles in both the traditional society and the existing one. Probably a majority of Yukon families find themselves together in the same band, although the band designation in most cases is a Whiteman's name. At the same time, a great many odd situations have developed, which provide considerable amusement: two brothers found themselves chiefs of separate bands although they had for years lived across the lake from each other; a northern Kutchin who was "staying" in the southern Yukon for a while to work on the highway found himself a member of a predominantly Tlingit band.

Less amusing and more important was the emphasis placed upon "legitimacy" of birth and the emerging importance of establishing illegitimacy when the father had been a Whiteman and the family wished to remain Indian. Several relationships that could have led to relatively stable families were quietly dissolved. Possibly most important of all was the final and irrevocable loss of Indian names. The government made no effort to discover or preserve any Indian identity. Only English names were taken—often reduplicated when only one was available (Joe Joseph, Tommy Thomas, Jimmy James)—and the all-important number was attached for ultimate government identification.

The bands and councils are largely nonfunctional sets of names existing only on paper. Occasionally an Indian agency superintendent will call a "council meeting" to sound out public reaction to an idea for housing assistance, or to a selection of candidates for schooling, or to an allocation of relief work such as cutting firewood for pensioners. Such groups and the individuals within them have no decision-making powers; the superintendent makes the decisions and most often he does so without consulting anyone.

All important interactions between Indians and the Yukon Indian Agency are unilateral, each individual taking care of his own problems with the government. These interactions are most often requests for help of one form or another from the Indian, followed by investigative queries from the agency worker. Agency decisions are completely paternalistic, without even a pretense being made of Indian participation in policy-level decisions. The superintendent is the ultimate authority in all matters (other than criminal offenses and torts). Indians who feel unjustly treated have no appeal—or at least know of no way to make such an appeal.

Occasional superintendents have been genuinely popular, but most relationships between them and the Indians are distant and marked by suspicion. The majority of Indians have some grievance—real or imagined—and usually approach the agency office with the expectation of being refused. Most agency personnel suspect that scheming Indians are trying to put something over on them. Faced with this background and attitude, the Indians have little alternative but to scheme means of "putting over" whatever matter they believe has to be taken to the agency office. (In defense of the agency personnel, however, it should be noted that a small segment of the urban Indian population is highly skilled at devising new means of obtaining a few dollars for Saturday night booze.)

The Whiteman government of the Yukon Territory moves in another orbit. An elected territorial council (with no provision for Indian representation) advises an Ottawa-appointed commissioner who is the ultimate local authority. The YIA superintendent attends weekly staff meetings with the commissioner, and some degree of coordination for Indian affairs results. Neither commissioner nor superintendent has authority over the other, however for either operation or planning. They operate on separate, parallel channels from Ottawa. Any Territorial services provided to Indians—health, welfare, institutionalizing—are separately accounted for and financed by the Indian Affairs Branch.

WHITEHORSE AND WHITEMEN

Indian perceptions of the Whiteman's world are based on the models available for observation within the Yukon Territory. Despite the new mobility offered by the Alaska Highway, few Indians have traveled "outside." Films, magazines, and the radio make available to Indians most of the existing Canadian culture, but the meanings they derive from such media are basically a function of direct observation. Practically all the goods and services available in Canada are available in Whitehorse and are utilized by some segments of the population. Although small in number, the population of the Yukon Territory probably reflects a genuine cross section of Canada's diverse total population. The city of Whitehorse dominates the Territory economically and socially. Whitehorse and its people are the prime models of Whiteman society to Yukon Indians.

Whitehorse has more of a metropolitan atmosphere than one expects from a city of little more than 4000 permanent inhabitants. Daily plane service and good communication facilities make it accessible, although seemingly remote. It is the center of government, financial, transportation, and storage facilities for the whole Territory. In the city are the only radio station, the only daily newspaper, and the only television station (closed subscription circuit) as well as army and air force garrisons with facilities for the dependent families (not included in the permanent population figures). The urban atmosphere is made complete by the presence of the only real slums in the Territory, populated by transient Indian and Whiteman squatters on Crown lands along the river.

Aside from government workers, the permanent business population, and armed forces personnel and their dependents, there is a continuous stream of developers and exploiters passing through Whitehorse. These are legal, technical, and scientific types, rather than the old-time prospectors and investors. They represent capital sources eager to invest in various known potentials; they are surveying, assessing, planning, negotiating, and in some cases already operating.

It is with another part of the Whiteman population however, that Indians have their most frequent social interaction. Socializing is done mostly in bars or, after closing times, in private homes where the parties begun in bars continue. The stable, middle-class Canadian society does not follow this pattern. The transient, semiskilled laborers who are found around most rapidly expanding areas do follow such patterns. To a segment of this population, work is the means to acquire sufficient capital for a prolonged binge. Some manage to acquire enough money to support a winter of calculated, alcoholic semistupor, during which they live in the cheapest accommodations available. Others blow what they have in a hurry, scrounge as long as possible, and then move on. Their comings and goings are almost continuous. Seldom noted, they remain approximately constant in absolute numbers. Many of this type of semiskilled worker stay in the Indian area of town in jerry-built shacks, sometimes living with an Indian woman as housekeeper and sometimes simply living alone because they share with Indians the attribute of being undesirable neighbors or companions to the more affluent Whitemen.

The other population segments can be identified in the usual Whiteman social role functions and classes. In terms of attitudes about and toward Indians, the groupings of the Whiteman population are not complex. Ronald Cohen (1962) characterizes three types of attitudinal syndromes among the non-Indian populations of the Mackenzie District communities in which he made a survey. Cohen's descriptions are apt for the attitudes observed in the Yukon, particularly the first two which, although not mutually exclusive, cover a great majority of the non-Indian population.

The traditionalists

These people feel that the non-White is basically a good man in his natural habitat, the bush, but that Euro-Canadian culture is making him depraved. Things were better in the old days when new ideas about "integration" had not yet become popular. In order that community life be run in an orderly and predictable fashion, local responsible Whites should make most of the major decisions because, ". . . they (non-Whites) are just like children." These people argue that because the whole region is poor economically, the non-White must get his living from the bush, and any modernization that moves him away from such a life is not only undermining him morally, but is unkind because it deprives him of a livelihood, and turns him into a relief case.

The apathetics

These people are egocentric. They often have liberal views about non-Whites, but are uncommitted to any policy of change or development in the region. They are pleasant, well-meaning, and are absorbed in their own jobs and social life, or do not intend to stay long in the north. They discuss northern problems but their views vary greatly about what is good and what is bad in the region, and they take practically no part in local affairs. Their main interests are the work situation, the home, and other White friends with whom they enjoy leisure time activities. The uses of community power are talked of, but never in terms of "me" or "us." Instead, wielders of local power are referred to as "they."

The new reformers

These people have absorbed the ideals of modern democracy and are convinced that their presence in the North means something in terms of human progress. Their personal viewpoint is the avowed policy of most senior civil servants in the area, although carriers of this viewpoint are rare at the local level. . . . They often feel isolated, frustrated, and in one place, two of them were resigning. . . . Those with more experience and calmer natures, who are willing to compromise with the traditionalists, form the core of the most valuable group of Whites in the region. Members of this kind of faction are interested in non-White participation in community affairs. They are willing to sacrifice efficiency and orderliness to a large extent, in order that non-Whites should be encouraged to take part in the decisions and activities of the community.

As Cohen suggests, the "new reformer" category is rare and in the Yukon is limited to a few civil servants plus a few teachers, an occasional missionary, and a tiny segment of Indians who have managed to penetrate Whiteman society to some extent. By and large, Whitehorse government and businessmen fall into the "tranditionalist" category, while the military and more transient of the new exploiters tend toward the "apathetic" characterization.

Among an interviewed segment of Whitehorse officialdom, certain responses illustrate these types as well as the prevailing attitudes that govern Whiteman-Indian relationships at this level.

A territorial-appointee administrator, a career civil servant on his way up and a man of action dedicated to progress and efficiency, affirms that official policy dictates "integration" of Indians. However, since there is no mechanism for Indian representation in government and since his social and official routine allows little time for exploratory activities or for direcct contact with Indians, his major support to this policy consists of urging facilitation of Indian children's attendance at public schools. The administrator hears advice from his staff and then makes firm decisions. His attitude is summed up by his words when a class of Indian children from the residential school visited his office one day. A question had been prepared in advance: "What *is* government?" He responded, beaming expansively: "Well, I guess you'd say *I'm* the government. . . ."

Agency administrators veer between official and verbal commitment to the reformer attitudes and a latent, traditionalist feeling that Indians are better off in the bush away from towns. "Whenever they ask me about enfranchisement, I tell them to forget about it," one assistant said. "They've got nothing to gain and everything to lose. . . . This is a lost generation, anyhow. There's no hope for them. They've got no leadership and no ability nor opportunity to practice leadership. We can get a few jobs for some of them, but they won't stick to them. It's the coming generation we have to work on. Maybe they'll be able to make it."

The agency men are so burdened with the bureaucratic details of providing aid for individual human tragedies, some of which are really almost beyond aid, that they have little time left for evaluating their professed ideals in operation. They seem to experience a deep sorrow that has to be somehow cloaked behind an almost callous disregard.

Police and court officials know Indians in a very special way. One elderly court appointee definitely attributes the "Indian problem" to the depravity that is forced upon them by Whitemen. Education and liquor discrimination are the two major problems, he says, and points out that during the preceding three years, Indians in Whitehorse court had paid over twenty thousand dollars in fines for liquor offenses that would not have been offenses had a non-Indian done the same thing. (These offenses were mostly possession or illegal consumption of liquor.)

And why do Indians drink as they do?

They lack values. It's the Whiteman's fault. It all comes from our urge to educate the whole population instead of taking only Indians who deserve education. Up here the Indian goes to school till he's sixteen, then he goes back to where he came from and the life he came from. Why? They haven't been taught any values . . . !

A constant stream of offenders in misdemeanor categories appears in court: about half are people of Indian ancestry, perhaps a third of the total are legal Indians. (Of ninety-two observed cases in a two-day period, fifty-one had Indian ancestry and twenty-nine were legally Indian. All those identified as Indian were involved in an offense concerning liquor.) It was observed that no Indian ever pled "not guilty" or had defense counsel, although non-Indians frequently said "not guilty" and a few brought lawyers with them. The court officer observed:

> They don't need lawyers. We provide for persons' rights and nobody is ever tried without knowing fully what his rights are. . . . No, I don't know of anything that is done to make people particularly aware of the law or of legal proceedings. We try our best from here and manage to get across a few lessons. Most people have a pretty good idea of what the law is. . . .

Very few adult Yukon Indians have not been in court at one time or another. When they are charged, it is the duty of a Crown prosecutor to present the case to the court. Crown prosecutors are Royal Canadian Mounted Policemen who take the prosecution duties on a rotation basis. They have no special training other than the meticulous training provided all members of their organization. A Crown prosecutor was interviewed just after the liquor laws had been changed to provide equal treatment for Indians and non-Indians: he was not optimistic about any lessening of police work as a result of the change in law.

> There'll be less trouble with possession and consumption, but we look for an increase in violent affairs; maybe even a murder or two each year and surely more on the "assault" level. Indians just aren't able to handle liquor. Already this year we've had four deaths from exposure while drunk. . . . But I'd rather have an Indian drunk than a White drunk. Indians aren't usually belligerent or abusive. They're much easier to handle. You just bring 'em in and let 'em sleep it off and they plead "guilty," pay their fine, and that's it. . . .
>
> They don't need counsel. That's *our* function. We enforce the *law;* we don't prosecute or persecute people. These people (Indians) are honest. They don't try to beat a charge like some Whites do. If they did something, they admit it. Most of them plead guilty right away. . . .
>
> No, I've never known Indians to call the police. They don't really need the police department. Indians are basically different . . . more honest than Whites. Once in a while there'll be a stolen rifle or snowshoes or something around a house, but they'll mostly handle their problems their own way. . . . This is really a very quiet town for police. Even these young men who are always hanging around (Indian) don't cause any trouble. Except we still find drunks wandering all over the place. Those are the ones we look for mostly. We just try to keep the lid on so they don't get into worse trouble. . . .

The territorial welfare office is similar to the Indian Agency office in that its personnel are overburdened with a multitude of tasks that never seem to be quite completed or quite as important as the next undone task. A caseworker says that the Territory's greatest problem is shared by Indians and non-Indians alike: the sparsity of community resources for coping with both normal and welfare needs. Historically, the Territory has been dependent upon neighboring provinces to provide institutional services for all its population. In postwar years its neighbor provinces have themselves experienced growth and are now unable to extend these services any longer to the Yukon. Therefore, problems of family guidance, legal aid, delinquency, and foster homes and adoptions are all but ignored in the Yukon.

> There's not a psychiatrist or psychiatric service available in the whole Territory . . . and, as for foster homes and adoptions, well, we have the legal machinery for it. We also have lots of homes—for White children. But we can't find homes to accept non-White children, regardless of legal status. . . .
> Proportionately, the non-White, non-Indian group [Indian ancestry but enfranchised] has the majority of welfare service. Unmarried Indian mothers take a big chunk of welfare money, but don't require much in the way of our services otherwise. They handle those situations among themselves. . . .
> But this "integration?" I feel the concept is sound, although the application is questionable. In elementary school it works all right, but there comes a period at high school age where discrimination almost invariably appears. Social life is very important at this age; dating begins and then come the tensions. Even when children are willing to date outside racial boundaries, parents most often object— White parents, that is. It's a bitter fact that social discrimination among adults reflects in children's behavior. Just look at the faces of Indian adolescents you meet on the streets—the sullen, almost defiant look. Our community teen-group organization is an excellent social device but very few Indians are involved. I have had Whitehorse teen-age Indians tell me time and again that they just can't feel easy at the club affairs. . . .

Another career civil servant is in charge of one of the large, modern hostels where most teen-age Indian children who attend school in Whitehorse live while going to school. (Full subsistence and a clothing allowance are provided.)

> I'm not an educationist; I've been a substitute parent to these Indian children. Why I even THINK like an Indian. . . . It's not unusual for non-Indians to request the privilege (of living at the Indian hostel while going to school when there is no school near their own home) but I find it impossible to acquiesce. . . . The hostel has had remarkable success in keeping teen-age young people at once happy and under control. The background of the Indian boys and girls at the hostel is such that our program is geared to control every element of their living. The minutest details are carried out under strict supervision. The secret of success in such a program in order not to offend any boy or girl is to be completely impartial. . . .
> I feel strongly about this because, on the one hand, I think I understand the native children reasonably well, and at the same time I have teen-age children of my own. I should not be willing to send MY children to a hostel such as this because of their different backgrounds. . . .

Public school administrators in the Yukon have had many problems resulting from rapid growth in recent years, only one of which has been the new policy of integrating Indian children into regular public schools wherever possible. Many new classrooms have been built, as well as some new schools; and the annual turnover in teaching personnel in the Yukon is now greater than the total teacher population was twenty-five years ago. One senior administrator who has been in the Territory through the entire period tries to be objective about Indian students:

> Other than basic integration where possible, we have no policy about Indian children. They come to school exactly as do other children. We have to maintain some separate records for Indian Affairs, but that's all. The children have the same

programs, the same facilities, and the same possibilities as any others when they're in public schools. Of course, you know, the majority still begin in the residential schools. . . . But there IS a problem. We know that. We're not holding Indian children in school. There's the same problem with White children but it's worse with Indians. We don't know what to do about it. Maybe the new vocational school will be part of the answer, but I think we have to go a lot further back than that. It's how they get started off that bothers me. They (Indian children) have things stacked against them from the beginning. Most of them spend an extra year or two in the first few grades because of language problems—they just haven't the vocabulary or patterns to comprehend—and then they get further and further behind and, by high school, they feel they're too old and they drop out. . . . No, it's a deeper problem than "guidance," or just more help in high school. Somehow we have to get children ready for grade one and off to a *start* in school that will permit them to maintain a more normal age-grade progression. . . .

A public health doctor whose work was mostly care of Indian and welfare patients expressed a prevailing sentiment among health practitioners of the Yukon. Doctors and dentists particularly prefer to have at least some private patients and they, particularly, take the brunt of Indian claims of need for support from the government, since all Indian medical care is provided free of charge to those who "cannot pay." Few people are willing to admit freely that they *can* pay.

I keep hearing them say they have the *right* to this or that . . . These people have no more rights than any other Canadian! The only Indian people with any rights that nobody else has are those under Saskatchewan Treaty number six who have a right to have a first aid box kept in the agent's house. And that's ALL! There's no justification for extending that symbolically to include every medical service—or every Indian in Canada. . . .

All the others are cared for by the benevolence of the government, and you have to watch that carefully. They'll abuse it. Why, I've had 'em drive up in Pontiacs and insist on glasses or false teeth to make 'em more beautiful. I tell 'em, "uhn-uhnnn! You buy your own, bud." Why, I had four girls sent here from Dawson for glasses. Twenty-one years old, they were. I asked 'em, "What work do you do? Nothing? What do you want glasses for? Do you read? What do you read? Love stories?! You go to movies? We'll not give you glasses to read love stories and go to movies! You do without glasses. . . ."

On the other hand, ya know, if they're sewing, trying to make some money or trying to better themselves, sure, we'll give 'em glasses. But we're not just going to make 'em look intelligent or pretty so they can pick up an extra two-and-six on the street or something. . . .

The children in school? Well, that's a different matter. We take care of them just automatically. It has to be done sooner or later anyhow. The parents, they don't really know. In their stage of development they can't understand what's right and what's wrong for kids. They don't really care, ya know? You hear about the close family relations of Indians. But they aren't really *close* families, these extended families you hear so much about. They are very loose families. More truly, they're collections of families that work more or less together, ya know, and children are shunted about from one to another without *any*body having *real* responsibility. We *have* to look out for them. . . .

Common to all these individuals, as to most of the non-Indian Yukon society, is a lack of contact or firsthand knowledge of Indians in their home communities. The impressions of the men quoted in this chapter are almost totally derived from work experiences in which interactions are structured by the role behaviors of the Whitemen in their official capacities. Informal social interactions—sharing of meals, visiting in homes, strolling on the street, attendance at the same public events—seldom involve Indians and Whitemen together. Exceptions occur among the lower level transient population, in which cases female Indians are seen with male non-Indians —never the reverse.

ORIGINS OF THE RESIDENTIAL SCHOOL AT MOPASS

The residential school has been at Mopass since its founding in 1901 by a bishop-missionary who dreamed of founding a new "see city" in the area. The few Indians still living who remember the bishop describe him and his plan in glowing terms and make references to how ". . . things might have been different if Bishop lived longer." He reportedly envisioned a church-supported, cooperative, community school-farm on the eighty-acre lakeside site where the school still operates.

Before his death three years later, the school was in existence and the church had provided a lay principal and several teachers. However, the new bishop was more interested in the main church development of the Yukon—the growing towns—and left the school to operate under the direction of a succession of principals. The farm principle was established and it continued until 1956 when the government as-sumed responsibility for Mopass's operation. However, the "community" concept never took hold. The school comprised grades one through eight; children worked half days and attended classes the other half days. A small cash budget was pro-vided by the church, but local collections plus the production of cows, chickens, and gardens were heavily relied upon. At the peak of its efficiency the Mopass school had over one hundred children and was very nearly self-supporting. Local hunters pro-vided moose and caribou. Farm production was largely milk, eggs, and root crops, but was enough for minimal needs. Older children cut firewood from the sur-rounding forest. It was not a particularly popular place; in fact, most of the persons who spoke of the school had memories that were more bitter than otherwise. Nev-ertheless, all Protestant Indians in the Yukon Territory who went to school at all during the first half of the twentieth century went to this school.

There is a certain amount of pride among Indians who have attended school. The pride is both that they themselves went to school and that school is available to their children. Despite all other feelings, school is still viewed by Indians as the avenue to social and economic advancement. They *want* their children in school and invari-ably give as their reasons some form of, ". . . so they can get a good job. You can't get no good jobs without education."

These positive inclinations are tempered by the many negative memories among adults, memories that are known to children and that form part of the children's expectations when they come to school as well as part of the parents' expectations of what school holds for their children, even though they know changes have been made. Tales of abuse are legion, abuse that is interpreted now as Whiteman prej-udice. Such tales are of different periods of time and involve different individuals. Dishonesty, cruelty, and sexual deviance or promiscuity are recurrent themes. Further inquiry almost invariably leads to memories of *good* teachers and valued learnings at the school, but these are seldom mentioned first. Typical anecdotes are:

> They sure didn't live their lives the way they preached. There was so much preju-dice it made me sick about religion. I never been much for church since them.

[This from a man who had spent five years at the school in the 1910–1915 era.]

> That principal was a crook. He made MONEY on that school! Know how I found out? I was there when he left and a new man came. Well, when I left, the new man figured up my account to pay me off. I'd been working as sort of supervisor on farm work and I'd cut some wood, too. Well, we was supposed to get paid for cutting that wood and the first man, he had been paying us a dollar a cord. When the new man figured it up, he paid me *two* dollars a cord. I said, "How come?" He said, "That's what you're supposed to get." Well, you know, that first crook, he'd been paying all us guys a dollar a cord and putting the other dollar in his pocket. . . .

Or, from an Indian who had been a student in the mid '20s:

> They starved us up there! We got one egg a year—at Easter. The rest of the time we got dogfood mush [corn meal] and skim milk. Them in the staff dining room, though, they got bacon and eggs every day. We never saw fruit from one Christmas to the next, but they sure had it. Why some of those kids just starved to death. One year there was six of 'em died right there at the school . . . starved to death!

Or

> That guy, he couldn't keep his hands off the girls. Up there at school and down here round town, too. He finally got kicked out, but he did all right for himself till then. He used to run a special boat over when the tourist trains were in town and he'd take a load of tourists down to the school. They he'd show 'em round and finish up by getting 'em all in the chapel for a service. His talk was always the same—you know, "It's better to *give* than *get*." Then he'd pass the collection around real fast. Man, what a take! Nothin' but bills. Big ones, too. But did we ever get decent food? Hah! Know what he'd do? He'd go down to the steamboats when they pulled in and he'd buy lard pails full of bacon drippings for two-bits a pail and that's what *we* spread on our bread!

Or

> I had a bad enough time at that school, but I learned to get along. I was smart and I could work. I got along all right. But when my kid was there, and they beat her up, that was too much. I finally took her out of there and got my franchise and sent her to town to school. I could have got that principal fired if I wanted to. He was a real crook, and a ladies' man, too. All the time fooling around down town here. And his wife was right up there at school. . . . They didn't feed them kids so good, you know, and I used to take my girl an orange now and then or something special, and he didn't like that. He was all the time finding out things she done and punishing her for it. Then one day he really beat her up and she ran away and came on down here. I went and told him she wasn't coming back and I was going to see the agent about how he was running things. But he apologized and said, "Let's forget about the whole thing." So I did. But she never went back there no more. He finally got fired anyhow. Clear fired. They kicked him clear outta the church. But he got a good job . . . anyhow. . . .

Over the years, the church's influence in school was recalled as more bad than good; and many Indians now prefer to see it entirely removed, although not at the cost of closing down the school. Indian attitudes toward school are as ambivalent as toward other Whiteman activities: in origin and in principle, school is good; in operation to date it has been not so good; however, it could and it should be good and is, in fact, getting better. Wait and see. It might turn out all right after all.

2 / The residential school operation

T HUS FAR, this case study has dealt with the history, composition, and attitudes of the broad community that is served or influenced by the residential school at Mopass. The ultimate objective is to examine the school closely as an environment in which learning takes place (Chapter 3). Before reaching that objective, however, the official, public, and casually observable operation of the school will be considered. The total community, including its history, might be considered the *learning context*. The actual school plant and its personnel as they function within it might be considered the *learning environment*.

THE PLANT FACILITY

The present residential school at Mopass was built by the Canadian government after fire had destroyed the church school in 1956. When the new school was put into operation, it came under the policy of "total government operation." This complex plan is a portion of the Canadian government's recent assumption of direct responsibility for the education of Indian children, with integration into Canadian society as the goal. The enforced separation of Indian children in public schools is now forbidden; direct subsidies are paid by the government to local public schools where Indian children are able to attend public schools; hostels are maintained near larger schools so that Indian children may attend public school upper grades when such schools are not within a reasonable distance of their houses. The residential school is maintained for younger children. It is believed that Indian primary school children should not have to adjust to both being away from home and being in the regular public schools for their first school experiences. The residential school also serves a welfare function for Indian children who do not, in the agency superintendent's opinion, have a "proper" home to live in while attending school.

In assuming responsibility for the operation of the residential schools, the government did not replace the churches; it simply assumed financial responsibility for the schools and guaranteed minimally trained teachers, while it left the church administrative hierarchy in control. This leads to a certain amount of competition among religious groups in the various schools. At Mopass the Anglicans eventually won the contract to continue their operation of the school because they had been longer established and are by far the majority and dominant Protestant group of the region. They are required to release non-Anglican children to other church personnel when parents so request, in order that all children may have regular religious

38

training while at school. Thus, to the historical significance of the school for the church, is added a sense of current urgency for its successful operation as a reflection of the church's ability to cope with changing conditions.

The Anglican Missionary Society of Canada is referred to as The Management in the government contract providing for operation of the school. A general handbook of directives guides each church-appointed principal in his operation of the school. Principals may be ministers or laymen; they are not professional educators.

Fixed formulas are established for food, clothing, transportation, and similar basic operating expenses. Within the budgetary and policy frameworks, each principal—and each church—is relatively free to operate independently. Procurement of

TABLE 1

COMPOSITION OF THE STUDENTS OF MOPASS INDIAN
RESIDENTIAL SCHOOL, 1962–1963

Age in 1962	Beginners		First		Second		Third		Fourth		Total	
	M*	F†	M	F	M	F	M	F	M	F	M	F
5	2	2									2	2
6	5	3									5	3
7	8	2	6	8	1	2					15	12
8	1	—	9	3	4	2	2	3			16	8
9					4	4	5	7			9	11
10					1	1	2	2	1	7	4	10
11							2	2	2	4	4	6
12							1	—	2	4	3	4
15									1	1	1	1
Totals	16	7	15	11	10	9	12	14	6	16	59	57

* M = male.
† F = female.

supplies and of nonteaching personnel are left entirely to their discretion. In addition to being allotted a specified portion of the school day to ". . . provide for religious and spiritual instruction . . . ," The Management is charged with the general "spiritual and religious welfare of the pupils. . . ."

The assignment of students to a residential school is the complete responsibility of the Indian agency superintendent. He makes the assignments on the criteria of family and child needs as determined by his staff; often he consults with local ministers before deciding, but seldom with residential school personnel.

The Mopass school is planned for 150 children at capacity. In 1962–1963, the school term the author taught there, 116 were attending in five graded classes. (See Table 1.) The category of "beginners" is recognition of most of the youngsters' need to acquire a common linguistic and conceptual background before they can move into the regular course of studies known as first grade. Compulsory attendance laws require school attendance from age six. The age distributions of these children reflect several deviant factors. The five-year-olds are from "family emergencies": foster homes are not available and the children must be placed somewhere. The eight-year-old beginners either "failed" their first year as beginners, failed a first year in public schools, or were neglected in their homes and not sent to school when agency personnel thought they would be. The continuing spread in ages results from the fact that most children in the school have failed one or more years either in the residential or in public schools. A few bright children move through the five-year residential school program in four years; a few more make it in five years; the majority require six or more years to move into fifth grade.

The school is located on an eighty-acre site bordering a lake about 2 miles from its nearest neighbor. About a third of the land is cleared and this portion slopes gently from the school to the lake shore. The plant is self-sufficient in an emergency; adequate storage and provisions for heat and electricity would enable the school to operate for a month or more in severe weather without anyone having to enter or leave.

The uncleared portion of the school grounds is "bush"—dense willow scrub along the shore line, merging into scrub spruce and jack pine away from the water. Both land and buildings are spatially separated into two categories: places where children *may* be and places where children may *not* be.

Children may play near the school, but not near the lake. They are forbidden to go alone into the bush, into fenced yards surrounding the houses of the principal and teachers, or into the garage and warehouse, which are adjacent but separate from the main building and have their own heating units. These restrictions are both for the children's safety and for the convenience of supervising personnel.

The four-story main building of reinforced concrete comprises the total living and working space aside from garage and warehouse. Fire precautions were an important consideration in its construction. There are no fire escapes, but four regularly spaced, enclosed stairwells with self-closing doors at each landing provide means of rapid exit from any place inside.

The first floor is about six feet above ground level. A semibasement is submerged so that its windows are at ground level. Entry into the main hall is up a flight of ten wide steps facing the lake, through double doors that lead directly to the chapel in the center of the structure. The principal's office and a staff lounge area are adjacent on either side of the entry. The remainder of the first floor consists of five classrooms, a teachers' workroom, four sleeping rooms for staff members, two staff lavatories and some storage closets. Children are never permitted on the main floor except by direction or under supervision.

On the basement floor, directly beneath the entry, is the kitchen and dining room. A storage and laundry space is behind, and an enclosed staff dining room opens from the children's dining room but is so arranged that the children cannot see inside. At each end of the basement floor are playrooms and toilets—one for boys and one for girls. Stairways lead from the playrooms to the upper-floor sleeping areas. The playrooms are probably the most familiar areas in the school to the children. The kitchen-dining room–laundry-storage complex is forbidden to children unless they are on duty there.

The fourth-grade group during recess in early spring. The Mopass Residential School is in the background.

The entire second floor comprises dormitories, equally divided between the sexes by a solid center partition. Each dormitory is a large open space with rows of lockers and beds, with small table by each bed. A partitioned room for a supervisor is in the center of each dormitory, dividing it into two sections known as junior and senior. These categories divide the children into age groups approximately above and below nine to ten years. Separate supervisors are in charge of junior and senior groups of each sex. Men never supervise girls; women often supervise boys.

The third floor consists of the staff living quarters, a nurse's office, and a four-bed isolation ward. Children are absolutely forbidden on the third floor unless sent to the nurse. Staff quarters are single cubicle rooms, each containing a cot bed, a wash basin, a chest of drawers, a chair, and a lamp.

The heating and auxiliary power plant are housed, along with an apartment for an engineer and his family, in a basement-level structure connected to the laundry by a narrow tunnel. Two low-pressure boilers provide steam heat and hot water; electricity comes from Whitehorse, and the auxiliary is for emergencies only. Children never go into the tunnel or to the boiler room.

For adults, the school is well laid out for functional operation. It is convenient, safe, and relatively comfortable. For children, it is comfortable but sharply segmented into those very few areas where they are relatively free at some times of the day; those places where they are regularly taken under direction for certain tasks; and those spaces (most of the plant) that are forbidden territory, awesome, mysterious, or unknown.

SCHOOL ROUTINES

The children come to Mopass School for ten months of each year. Usually they remain there the entire time. The government transports them to school in early September and takes them home again in late June or July by means of chartered buses. Aside from the proximity of three relatively "local" children, distances to the various homes range from a minimum of 50 miles to over 350.

Parents are required to pay the cost of Christmas or Easter vacation trips home; few do so. Routine cycles are established for efficient handling of the children and to provide both children and staff with a predictable living situation, which is intended to duplicate a home situation as nearly as possible. With the exception of the new students each year, the routines are well known to all the children.

As the buses roll into the schoolyard to discharge the road-weary children early in September, the school is ready for them. They are quickly fed, bathed, issued new clothing, and checked by the nurse. The atmosphere is one of subdued excitement; quick exchanges of greetings among the children, sizing up of new adult personnel, helping the new young children learn to fall into lines and stand at attention as necessary. Each child is given a complete issue of new clothing, including changes of underwear, stockings, shoes, overshoes, play clothes, school clothes, and Sunday clothes. (They take their clothes home at the end of the year and need not return or account for them.) Children with body lice have their hair cropped very close and are scrubbed with disinfectant. Work rosters have already been made up so that each child has some minor duties to perform. The days between the children's arrival and the beginning of classes are used for basic socialization—indoctrination of newcomers and re-establishment of routines for the returnees.

During the summer, the school has operated with a skeleton crew while staff vacations were taken and maintenance completed. A very few children have been at school all summer, having no homes to which they could go. It has been a quiet, drowsy time for them—a few chores each day, lots of free time, occasional chances to ride in cars or trucks on short trips, and no regular activities other than meals and sleep. Supply shipments have periodically arrived, and sorting these out for distribution or storage has been the biggest event of the summer. To these children particularly, resumption of routine and the return of the rest of the children is a welcome event.

The school year is divided into segments between holidays in such a manner that everybody, student and staff alike, can look forward to a major holiday event within six to eight weeks. These are used as motivators; as times for reward, for controlling behavior, and for providing the stuff of anticipatory daydreams. Thanksgiving is early in October, followed by Halloween, Christmas and Easter vacations and the end of school. After Christmas, a midwinter carnival day for outdoor sports provides a break before Easter; a similar spring sports day serves the same function between Easter and the end of scchool.

Teachers and supervisors have behavior expectations of the children geared to the holiday cycle. Christmas is a classic motivator, and the children are considered to be "at their best" until then. The time between Christmas and Easter is viewed by teachers as being the best instructional period. Excitement is not so intense as before Christmas, and those children who perform well academically have maximum interest and opportunity after Christmas. To supervisors, this same period is the one in which they expect the most serious behavior problems, because the Christmas motivation no longer operates to inhibit misbehavior and those children who are going to misbehave have been in the school long enough to have lost their awe at both the personnel and the plant. From Easter until the end of school, it is commonly felt by both teachers and supervisors that one just "keeps the lid on." With the coming of spring and the prospect of summer vacation, it is said to be just too much to expect good performance from the children.

The weather does, indeed, reinforce such a cycle. The winter's snow is on the ground by early November and the lakes are frozen. Snow, ice, and subfreezing temperatures (from 20 degrees above to 60 degrees below zero) will prevail until mid-April of the following year. Daylight in mid-December lasts a scant four hours, with the sun barely appearing above the horizon. A high percentage of winter days are cloudy, stormy, and dark and even further reduce outdoor activity potential. At such times, although the shelter of a warm building is appreciated by anyone who happens to be outdoors, confinement within a restricted space along with 150 other individuals has a certain depressing effect, from which some behavior abnormalities can be expected.

The other extreme of the weather cycle also has its sense of confinement. As spring comes, the days lengthen until there is nearly no darkness at all. Windows are fitted with heavy black-out curtains, but the children have increasing difficulty getting to sleep after the first of May. The arrival of new flocks of birds and the honking of geese overhead can generate great flurries of excitement. Going home becomes the universal topic of conversation—even among those who know they must remain at school during the summer.

The final week of school is a hectic period of packing, cleaning, health checks, and many good-bys and plans for maintaining contact during the summer. The principal interviews the few children who are not to leave. This brings a period of tears and withdrawal behavior among them until final good-bys are said as the last bus departs, after which those remaining fit into the modified daily and weekly routines as the school drowses through another summer, awaiting the beginning of a new cycle the following September.

The children's weekly school cycle involves classroom and nonclassroom events, the latter divided into free time and work or church events. Different behaviors and dress are required for each of these activities. Sunday is a unique and climactic day. Learning the appropriate behavior and appearance for the various activities is one of the first socialization tasks set new students.

Classes normally operate from 9 A.M. till 3:30 P.M., Monday through Friday. The older children rotate domestic duties on a monthly basis, with crews in the kitchen, laundry, and dining room, or busy at cleaning dormitories and so forth. All this work, except kitchen chores, is done before classes and on Saturdays. Various evenings are set aside for special interest groups—Cub Scouts, Girl Guides—but most evenings are simply spent quietly playing or reading until time for bed. Friday night is a time when the staff people make the hundred-mile round trip to town for shopping and movies, with a minimum staff left behind at the school. On that night children usually have a special cocoa and cookie treat before bed.

Saturday mornings are work times; afternoons are for free play; and evenings, for the movie that is held in the chapel-auditorium and is open to public attendance. Children from nearby settlements attend the movie free of charge; from twenty to fifty outside adults usually attend and pay a fee of 50 cents. Residential school children sit separate from the others, arriving and departing in groups, and under supervision as at all other activities.

Sunday, church day, begins with the school's rising half an hour later than on other days. No work is done except in the kitchen. Religious services begin with Sunday School for junior students, followed by a regular church service either in the chapel or in the local settlement church. If the latter is the site, the older children are transported the 3 miles in school vehicles. A big noon meal follows church services, and the afternoon is for free but subdued play.

The twenty or so Baptist children create somewhat of a problem each Sunday. Although there are no Baptist residents nearby, that church maintains a mission in the settlement just to provide Sunday services for the residential school children. While Anglicans disapprove of the arrangement, they have no alternative but to cooperate to the extent of releasing the children since this is part of the contract. Supervisors are not at all gracious about the task of specially preparing a small group of their children to go off to the Baptist mission each Sunday. In former years, the principal had stood at the school doorway as the Baptist children returned and he had confiscated the small bits of church literature, pictures, and so forth which the children brought back. In 1962 this practice was discontinued.

On single-day holidays, the Sunday routine usually prevails; on longer holidays, the Saturday routine is followed. Except for Saturday and Sunday events, the daily routine is almost invariable.

Each event (including those on Saturday and Sunday) is preceded by a toot of the police whistle that each supervisor carries. This commands initial attention; a shouted command from the supervisor conveys the message.

The children are awakened at 6:30 A.M. to rise, wash, dress, and make their beds. They do not dress in school clothes yet; morning cleaning chores and breakfast require play clothing—jeans and shirts. Breakfast is at 7:30; the children on dining room and kitchen duty eat half an hour earlier. The supervisor's first task is to get them under way on time. Then the other children are gradually moved downstairs to the playroom adjacent to the dining room. Five minutes before mealtime the children are in lines in the playrooms, waiting quietly. At a signal from the supervisor they fold their hands in prayer position and repeat a grace prayer in unison. This saves time and avoids the problem of getting their attention while they are actually seated at the dining tables.

Soon after the prayer ends, the doors are opened by the dining room supervisor and the children file quietly to their preassigned places at the tables. Girls and boys sit at separate tables in separate sections. A senior student, one at the head of each table, is responsible for setting behavior standards for the eight other children, four on each side. Placement of the children is by age and friendship groups, at the discretion of supervisors.

The food is ready to be eaten at each child's place when the children enter; more is brought by attendants as required. No child moves from his place during the meal, and each is encouraged to eat his fill, particularly of milk, fruit, and protein foods. Consumption of bread and other starches is controlled by requiring the total balanced diet to be consumed before supplementary foods are provided, but no limit is imposed on the amount of food available.

One adult boys' supervisor and one girls' supervisor sit and watch from opposite ends of the dining room, seldom interfering with the meal except to assist when a problem arises or to intercede in case of argument. Such assistance or intercession is infrequent.

The children at each table remain there until all at the table are finished. At that time, the senior student of the table signals the supervisor who checks to see that all have eaten properly and are finished, then gives a signal for them to leave. The senior student leads the others in a short prayer, then leads the students in line out to their playrooms. Conversation in the dining room is minimal and subdued at all times, in sharp contrast with the playrooms and dormitories.

When everyone is finished eating and has reassembled in the playroom, the children return to their dormitories to complete undone tasks. By 8 A.M. all are expected to be changing into school clothing. All the clothing is similar, but not necessarily uniform. Junior girls and boys are dressed alike each day; older ones are permitted to select their choices of several shirt or dress colors available. Boys wear corduroy or cotton slacks, pull-over or flannel button-down shirts, and oxford shoes. Girls' school clothing is cotton-print dresses in ten or twelve simple styles and colors, ankle socks, and oxford saddle shoes.

By 8:30 all members are expected to be ready for chapel, which begins at 8:45. They are inspected by their supervisor as they assemble at the stairway to the lower hall. Between 8:35 and 8:40 the children file slowly down to the first floor hall and along to the chapel. Complete silence is the rule for this passage and for presence in the chapel. At 8:45 the principal (or vice-principal or visiting minister) and organist enter, and music begins a typical morning ceremony. The minister stands at the pulpit in an attitude of silent prayer. After a short silence, he announces a hymn number. All rise and sing the hymn, adult female voices carrying the burden and dominating. (All employees attend chapel.) At the conclusion of the song, all are seated and the minister announces the topic referent for his day's message. He reads a bit from his book, then makes a short interpretation of the direct relevance of the message for his audience. He concludes by announcing another hymn. All rise and sing again, after which they remain standing with heads bowed while the minister leads another prayer. The chapel ceremony is then completed, and everybody sits while the principal pulls closed a large stage curtain that hides the altar and pulpit and thereby converts the chapel into the auditorium. Messages and announcements are then made; often the message has to do with behavior or rule infractions. When the principal signals that he is finished, supervisors direct the children into lines for passing to classrooms, smallest children first. It is now about 9 A.M. The rule of silence prevails, but a hum of conversation and muffled laughter is already beginning as the children near their classrooms and the takeover of teacher authority. At that time, supervisors are officially relieved by the teachers in charge of the students.

Each classroom is designated as a grade room. Children of that grade stay in the rooms for all lessons. A fifteen-minute recess comes at 10:30 A.M. One teacher has recess duty for each sex. Toilets for children are located only in the dormitories or in ground floor playrooms, and the boys and girls must go in line to their respective playrooms at each recess, with the lines from some rooms passing each other as they go the full length of the building. At the end of recess the lines move back to the classrooms.

Noon dismissal is at 11:45. Supervisors appear in the hallways outside the classrooms to take charge of the children and prepare them for 12:10 lunch. Again the children move in single file, this time to their dormitories where they wash and repeat the morning meal routine. After lunch, the younger children go to the dormi-

Two school girls, beginner and second-grader. Their dress and appearance are typical.

tories to rest; older children go outdoors, or to playrooms, until 12:50 when they reassemble to pass in line to the classrooms. Teachers are free during the noon period and take charge of children again at 1:00 P.M. Afternoon classes continue until 3:30, with a recess at 2:00 following the pattern of morning recess. Beginners and first grades are released at 3:00. At class dismissal, all children go in line to their dormitories where they immediately change clothes. Unless they have an evening duty, they are free to play until 5:00 when all reassemble in the dormitories to wash and prepare for the evening meal at 5:30. Again the meal routine is the same. By 6:00, dinner is over and within the next half-hour the kitchen is cleared and the children on that duty are also free.

Two nights a week are bath nights when all children bathe under supervision and with the help of designated "scrubbers" who use soap liberally on backs, ears, and so forth. On nonbath nights all that is required is simple face, hand, and teeth washing, although the children may take extra baths if they request them. All children wear flannel pajamas or nightgowns to sleep, and each child has his own separate bed. The junior children are in their beds soon after 7:30; the older children, at about 8:00. After prayers, they are usually asleep by 8:30; and the supervisors are then free to assemble in the staff lounge, visit elsewhere in the school, or pursue individual interests in their own rooms (provided one is always near each dormitory).

Although days are organized on strict time segmentations—particularly for meals and classes—there is only one clock in the school. It is located on the wall over the principal's door in the main hall, an area forbidden to the children. Most adults have wrist watches; none of the children have watches and few of them can tell time. Aside from the central fire-alarm signal, there is no bell system. The supervisor's police whistle thus assumes an even greater regulatory significance in the children's lives. They know, at any given time, what the next whistle will indicate; they know, too, that it will be blown well in advance of the required time for the event. The whistles are shrill and urgent. Responses do not match the intended urgency. The children appear to resent—consciously or unconsciously—the ubiquitous whistles and the insistent tone of the repeated blasts. Typical is an observation of a group of thirty boys playing at various places in the ten-acre field beside the school:

> 4:55 P.M. S has been sitting on a bench by the garage while the boys play. Now S blows the whistle, three long blasts. Several of the nearer boys look up at S and then rise and begin dusting off their hands. Most of the boys seem not to hear and continue their activities. S shouts, "Hey, you senior boys!" and blows the whistle twice more, "Time to come in for supper." Most boys stop what they are doing. They know supper is a good half-hour away. A slow drift of the group toward the supervisor begins. Six of the boys furthest away near the woods continue their game. S blows again, twice, and shouts, "You boys come, right this instant!" Two more blasts on the whistle. The boys nearest S begin to run. Others move a bit more rapidly but do not begin to run until they are so near that S could possibly chase and catch them. The six boys in the distance stop their play and begin walking slowly. S blows another long blast. Half the boys are now in the playroom; all others except the six laggards begin to run. "You Charles! Come ON. Hurry UP!" The six by now are quite near to S and are the last to be outside. They begin to run. As they pass near, S makes a swipe as if to spank one of them, but he ducks aside and runs on into the playroom. S follows. The whistle blasts repeatedly within the playroom in an attempt to silence the hubub. . . . 5:10 P.M.

This pattern is repeatedly observed among both boys and girls. Those nearest the supervisor when the whistle blows tend to move smartly; any threatening possibilities diminish directly with distance from the supervisor, so that being 100 feet away is quite safe. Yet it is always necessary to pass fairly close by the supervisor in order to do what must be done, so that highly responsive behavior has to be displayed at the right moment—the moment the child perceives as the one of highest danger potential. This is not a function of the same individuals being the farthest away all the time, but a function of perceived compulsion in direct relation to physical proximity to the authority figure. The situation is highly frustrating to supervisors, who continually repeat futile efforts to get children to understand that the *farther* away they are, the *faster* they should come.

THE RESIDENTIAL SCHOOL CURRICULUM

To discuss curriculum in the residential schools, one must all too rapidly cut through several levels of abstraction, proceeding downward from ideal statements to operational reality. Indian Affairs Branch official policy statements are well-written documents in which curriculum is viewed as the total experience of the child at school, in the classrooms and outside. Objectives are stated in terms of bridging two cultures and furthering integration. Guidance and supervision in the total living experience are considered integral portions of a single, over-all curriculum.

Unfortunately, the policy becomes nonoperational with the following statement found in the *Indian School Bulletin* (January 1957):

> The appropriate provincial course of studies will be used in all Indian schools and interpreted in light of the philosophy upon which it is based. Adjustments to the programme which do not come within its framework, such as the addition of new courses or the curtailment of courses, etc., will be undertaken only with the consent of the regional inspector of schools. . . .

Since the Yukon schools have never developed their own curriculum statement, the "appropriate provincial course of studies" has been a direct adoption of the British Columbia *Programme of Studies for Elementary Schools* (Province of British Columbia 1960). This basic curriculum document, whose form is familiar to all educators, is complete with prescriptive statements and "suggested" time allocations for the various subjects.

The Yukon Territory supplements this document with a territorial *Manual for Teachers,* which is prepared annually to state teacher working conditions, inspection and report procedures, and so on. Neither document contains any reference to Indian children or Indian schools, or to adaptations for singular cases. Both documents emphasize systematic instruction in tool skills, the necessity for schedules and time allocations, and an essential program of testing. The superintendent of territorial schools in the Yukon is delegated as local inspector of Yukon Indian Schools.[3]

A justifiable inference from the published Indian Affairs Branch policy is that its general objectives and the guidance and curriculum experiences of Indian children are a concern of all who are in official contact with them during their school life. In residential school practice, curriculum and guidance are narrowly viewed and are generally held to be the separate domains of teacher (curriculum) and supervisor (guidance). The published materials are available to all but it is doubtful that many employees of the school read them; more doubtful, even, that their meanings are conveyed to those who do read them. "That's good stuff, but pretty heavy in theory for us," the principal once commented after reading a guidance statement that had been recommended as relevant for all staff members.

---

[3] It should be made explicit that the policy of integration is thoroughly accepted in principle among schools of the Yukon. Nothing except conscientious effort to implement this policy was ever observed, from top government levels where decisions are made about new classrooms and more teachers, to the teachers themselves in the classrooms. However, an invariable assumption operates among non-Indians that Indian children, to be integrated, must have the *same* education, the same services, and must pass the same tests in order to be considered to have completed the various grade levels of schooling.

At the level of provincial and territorial manuals, the prescriptions are obviously meant for teachers in the classrooms of day schools. Thus there is little potential for the use of such materials among a joint teacher-supervisory staff of a residential school. A rigid, subject-oriented course of studies is encouraged by employment policies and by policies regulating the provision of texts.

Residential school teachers are the products of a highly centralized system that includes teacher-training channels for non-Indian public schools. No teacher at Mopass had been trained in any other field of study. Their expectations when arriving at the school are that Indian children should perform with about the same materials and at about the same conceptual levels as the lower-class levels (because of "home conditions" and "language problems") among the population they had been trained to teach.

All textbooks are procured by order from a standard list supplied by a government printing office in Ottawa. The lists consist of single sets of texts adopted for each subject. No variations or supplements are offered among the basic texts. Additional and supplementary text materials are usually approved when requested from the regional office. However, the initiation of such requests is strictly the responsibility of the teacher. Operating against such initiative (deviation) is first the teacher's own lack of background information about the materials available and, in addition, the policy directive that any adjustment of the program be undertaken ". . . only with the consent of the regional inspector of schools." (See extract from the *Indian School Bulletin*.) It is an unusual teacher who perseveres through the process of developing his own adjustments, then going through the procedure of justifying them for the approval of the regional inspector, and, finally, spending additional time making out supplementary requisition orders. At Mopass, the first grade teacher expressed amazement and delight when, after her pupils had finished the prescribed texts in April, she was given permission to duplicate supplementary text materials from another source. She said that she would usually expect to be told to repeat and review the completed text materials.

Generally, teachers grasp at a discrete element of curriculum policy such as the aim " . . . to develop readiness for systematic learning of the essential tools of thought and communication . . ."; and these isolated objectives become their operating framework. The remainder of the various policy directives and suggestions are largely ignored, except those having to do with specific accountability and record-keeping of materials. As prescribed, timetables are drawn up for the various subjects; and instruction centers around reading, writing, and arithmetic, with the first of these featuring Dick, Jane, Spot, Puff, and the all-too-familiar friends, neighbors, pathways and streets of both Canadian and United States textbooks. A heavy reliance upon church and folk music and upon color crayon drawing provides basic relief from daily repetitions of book assignments in skill subjects.

Testing policies—and, in some cases, even basic record-keeping—are ignored. A permanent record card is made for each child. It is devised to provide final course grades and certain test results over his twelve years of public schooling. At the Mopass school, none of the prescribed diagnostic or achievement tests had been given to the children at any level. Indeed, the information on students' permanent record cards was scanty and confusing. Many children had completed grades with satisfactory marks, but had then been overlooked and required to repeat that grade the following year. Other children had been at the school one or two years before any card was made or any record kept of their attendance. Still others had unexplained gaps of a year in their record cards. (An unconfirmed report was that previous school authorities had adhered to the policy that any child who "failed" would have *no* entries made on his permanent record card. No personnel remained at the school who could confirm the report.) A single numerical entry per subject per year is the total information available about the children in the school in regard to both their academic performance and classroom behavior.

Evaluative information is derived exclusively by each teacher from his own instructional procedures. Neither school procedures nor the final numerical grades provide any reflection of the "bridging two cultures" concept of Indian Affairs Branch official curriculum policies. A stranger viewing the school in operation would have difficulty finding any indication, other than the facial features of the pupils, that he was among a non-Anglo culture group.

Guidance efforts on the part of the teachers are not encouraged by the structure of administrative- and staff-teacher relationships at the residential school. Staff is operationally defined as the nonprofessional teachers. The church employees are the *staff;* the *teachers* are government employees. School policy strictly prohibits "interference" by anyone other than the person in charge of the children at any given time. When teachers work, the supervisors are not working, and vice versa. Effective, concerted guidance efforts would require shared understandings and purposes as well as the close, positive relationships that are just not obtained when the physical possibilities of interaction are few.

The matter of students being overlooked and required to repeat a year is illustrative. No records indicated the reasons; moreover, although several supervisors had been at the school for five years prior to 1962 and thought it was "too bad" in at least some cases, they had no idea why some children had been made to repeat grades. Each person at work is primarily concerned with accomplishing his own task, be it care of the children, instructing them, or accomplishing work with the children's labor. A secondary consideration is avoiding conflicts with other adults who later interact with the children. The psychological processes of individual children are a poor third consideration. Only very overt disruptive behavior brings the various adults together to consult about a given child.

"Guidance" is thus largely a function of implicit understandings derived by the children from their own observation of adult models. The staff's performance criteria are in terms of group behavior. A group that "cooperates" and makes no problems is left alone; individuals who disturb are given a talking to or punishments and, generally, a disproportionate share of attention. Physical punishment is not used in the classrooms or by the principal (although until recently all teachers had kept straps and had used them liberally), but it is used by supervisors and vice-principal (although rarely) and provides a constant ultimate threat for some children. All behavior problems requiring official attention are taken to the principal or vice-principal. Nobody considers it proper to refer a problem to the teachers. In spite of their relatively high status, the teachers are not considered either authority figures or guidance personnel by the children or the church staff.

COMMUNITY RELATIONS

As an institution of the local community, the residential school has religious and economic significance beyond its educational function. For the nearby settlements, it is the center of church activities of all kinds and not only of Sunday services. To all the Anglicans of the area, it is a symbol of the contribution their church has made and a reaffirmation of the church's continuing importance to territorial development. The school provides direct income to employees, to storekeepers, and to transportation facility workers. An additional—although incalculable—economic input to the territory from the school is the provision of food, clothing, and incidentals to over 100 children per year whose families would otherwise be supporting them.

The community approves unequivocally of the school only in general terms. Such approval does not extend to the individuals who operate the school. The experiences of over fifty years have resulted in attitudes of suspicion toward the various roles represented by staff and teacher personnel. There is a tentative willingness to accept them in the community as positive elements, but a concurrent necessity to have this demonstrated.

Mopass School had a new principal in 1962. He set a first priority upon establishing good relationships with the local communities, and it was frequently said by local residents that town-school relationships were the best ever that year. Salient in the memories of all, for comparative purposes, were the years immediately preceding during which an autocratic, arbitrary, and rigid personality had dominated the school until he was dismissed at the end of the previous school year. (Most frequent criticisms of the former man were on the order of: "He wouldn't say burial service for J S when he killed hisself." "He refused to marry J cause she'd been divorced." "He wouldn't allow no Indian to ride in his car no matter what. He said theys all the time fartin'.")

The community comparison level for positive acceptance is not high. As is common in many small towns, individual personal idiosyncrasies are intimately known, tolerance for such is rather high, and the tendencies are toward friendly relations with strangers. Thus, absence of sexual deviance, relative honesty, and a minimum willingness to communicate are sufficient attributes for acceptance in the small Yukon community (and the first two are not extremely important if the last trait is adequately demonstrated).

Reversing a previous policy, the new principal hired as many local people as was possible. He also made some changes in procurement procedures in order to give more business to local firms, encouraged the church's Women's Auxiliary unit to use the school for regular meetings, and instituted a series of weekly social hours for the adults of the community. Thus, most of the non-Indian adults within reasonable driving distance are in one way or another involved with the school, with the degrees of involvement ranging from direct economic relation to occasional attendance at the weekly movie. The general feeling about the principal was expressed as " . . . He's a good, hard-headed businessman. No nonsense about him." This reflected both his efficient business operation and his politic distribution of patronage.

A large segment of the local Indian population does not participate in the social hours or other activities of the school—the same segment that seldom participates in any community activities of any kind. Among them is a strong latent feeling of grievance, stemming from past experiences, that simply will not permit them to accept any overtures for close relationships from school-church personnel. The Indians who did participate were mostly the families of those employed on the staff. No parents of the students at the residential school were ever involved in the social events there.

In many places, and to many people, the principal extended invitations to visit the school, to take meals there, to spend the night. These were accepted by quite a few people having "status" in the community. His invitations were never extended to Indians.

No non-Indian on the 1962 staff was personally acquainted with any Indians other than former students and the families of those Indians on the staff. Contacts with parents are limited to the very infrequent visits of parents to the school and the times when students are picked up or returned home. At such interactions the behavior norms of parents and the school staff are so extremely dissimilar that little more than cursory greetings are exchanged.

A visit by parents to the school is unexpected and uncomfortable. The staff knows that many children are welfare cases and has heard lurid tales of drunkenness, sexual promiscuity, and family neglect about various parents. No records are available to show which families are in such categories and which have children in the school simply because the family home is remote. The staff therefore tends to assume that the visitor is of the dissolute category and is not inclined to accord the visitor the same respect that a non-Indian parent might expect during a visit to a regular public school.

The visitor has come to school in a taxi or a friend's car. He is seated on a bench in the open hallway outside the chapel, and the child or children to be visited are brought to stand before the visitor during the interaction. Children are always eager to see visitors, but their usual behavior when in the actual presence of the visitor is to stand with head hung or averted. The visitor hugs the child and repeats its name several times, then sits and talks intermittently until the cumulative discomfort becomes intolerable and the visit ends with another hug, a few pats, and admonitions to be good and to write letters. Parents seem pleased to see their children, but a little bewildered and embarrassed at the avoidance responses of the children.

The interview becomes particularly critical if a staff member or teacher approaches. Parents seem to expect criticism of either themselves or their children, or both. They are relieved if no criticism is forthcoming, but then try to be so very agreeable and are so eager to please the school person that a comfortable discussion of the child's background or behavior in realistic terms is impossible. Aside from smiles and nodding of the head, responses are minimal. One soon begins to feel like an intruder and, realizing that he is misusing time during which the parent and child could be visiting, retreats from their presence. In such situations the avoidance behavior of the children increases the tension. They become very uncomfortable, never respond verbally, and often exhibit extreme behavior such as turning to face another

*Avoidance behavior during picture-taking. The girl holding the string game is the
sixteen-year-old for whom there is no record of her early years at the Mopass school.*

direction, twisting their hands, sometimes crying, and at best mustering a grimmac-
ing smile beneath the hung head.

(I feel that children in these situations are unable to reconcile their dual identities. A child's school identity as an unobtrusive group member is inconsistent with
his family identity as an accepted, if peripheral, individual. Nothing in his life experience either at home or at school has equipped him to be a center of attention.
Much as the child may feel a need for attention from both relatives and school personnel, he has no acceptable behavior patterns available for expressing this need.)

Most school staff members say that Indian parents fall into two categories: those
who realize that the residential school provides much more than the family can provide and who are pleased to have their children so well cared for; and those who do
not care much, one way or the other. In any case, the staff maintains, children are
much better off in the school than they would be at home. Staff members often cite
the behavior observed at parents' infrequent visits to substantiate their conclusions.
"Why, when her mother visited, that child could hardly stand to be near her! What
kind of a life would she have at home?"

Among Indian parents there are probably examples of both the attitudes attributed to them. However, most parents seem to prefer that their children stay at home
to attend school, but are under the impression that they have no choice other than to
designate their children as Catholic or as one of the Protestant faiths in order to determine which of the two residential schools they will attend. To a large extent, the
parents are correct. No known effort is recorded or recalled by either Indian or

non-Indian official personnel of attempts to involve Indian parents in any phase of decision-making about policy for the education of their children.

Acting in an outright paternalistic manner, Yukon Indian Agency personnel sometimes use children in their efforts to influence families. Sometimes children are removed from their homes and placed in residential school because of neglect on the part of the parents who are told that the children will be allowed to stay at home if the parents "straighten up." At other times, reluctant parents have been forced to keep their children at home to attend public school because the agency felt that the sense of responsibility for the children's welfare would have a stabilizing effect upon a disintegrating family situation. These situations are, of course, publicly known as is the fact that the decisions are made by the agency, not by the families.

Not only does Mopass Indian Residential School policy lack any reflection of Indian attitudes, heritage, and perceived needs, but furthermore there is literally no communication between Indian parents and the Whitemen educators about the children's growth in school. Evidence is seen of vague desires on the part of both to have some sort of communication; but there is neither policy nor administrative machinery within which to achieve this end, and the administration is unable to function without such directives. Children perceive the impossiblity of such communication, although probably without being able to verbalize it. It makes them very uncomfortable to have their parents or family around the school.

SUMMARY OF SCHOOL OPERATION AT MOPASS

The children are well housed, clothed, fed, and cared for in a remote, self-contained school that is a living unit as well. Life in the school is group life. Aside from a few play situations, the life of a child at the Mopass school affords him few occasions to have a dyadic relationship with any individual, unless he is in trouble— a condition to be avoided if possible. His life span within school is spent as a member of a group (preferably inconspicuous) that is involved in a cyclical series of predictable events. One learns to obey directives from authorities and, at the same time, to subordinate tendencies toward autonomous behavior. Adult models reinforce this tendency, since status-derived authority is highly important among the adults of the school.

A general statement about initial reactions to any given situation by both children and adults might be that they first consider, "What authority have I to . . . ?" rather than something in the nature of "What *should* be done about . . . ?" Among children, this more frequently takes the form of "Who said . . . ?" an almost invariable response to any directive. The genesis of this pervasive response tendency is obscure, but the pattern is reinforced by the fact that *every* activity in the school is directed by someone. It is further reinforced by the nature of governmental operations within extended bureaucracies, a nature exuding the concept of line authority from top to bottom. Conceivably this authority dependency could also be a latent function of church-missionary relationships, or a carry-over compensation mechanism of the European immigrant population that is dominant in Yukon business and government structures, but basically insecure within the total Canadian society.

Regardless of its source, such authority is both sharply segmented among several adult groups and jealously guarded, nurtured, and reaffirmed in almost any possible manner.

At the staff level, the principal is the final authority. Each individual relates himself directly to the principal, regardless of the necessity of taking working directions from others. The vice-principal is in charge of the kitchen and cleaning crews. However, when those employees are unhappy about any aspect of the vice-principal's operation, they go directly to the principal. Early in the year, when questioned about a situation that had taken an unhappy turn, a supervisor told the principal, "Well, I told Mr. [vice-principal] . . . " The principal did not accept this. "You should have told *me!* I want to know about these things." He repeatedly said that he wanted "democratic relationships," and he prides himself that he is always available to hear any grievances. Whenever complaints come to him, he takes prompt action to satisfy them and maintains daily and weekly checks in such a manner that their is no doubt about his being in control.

For all his apparent power, however, the principal in turn derives his authority from a carefully outlined documentation of functions in his handbook. He can cite a documented source for every activity, and for every failure to act. Thus he can, and did, order thousands of dollars worth of clothing and food entirely at his own discretion from suppliers of his own choice; but he cannot order needed indoor play equipment because handbook directives refer only to *out*door play equipment. He can dispatch a school vehicle almost anywhere for any purpose, with or without children in it; but he cannot allow children to ride in such vehicles if they are on their way home for holidays because a directive forbids it. He is charged with the total welfare of the children for a ten-month period, but he has no choice in the selection of his students. Although he expressed an awareness of the need for closer relationships with the adult Indian population and for a reflection of Indian attitudes and aspirations in the formation of policies at the school, he made no attempts to do this because there are no handbook procedures for the purpose.

In functional terms, supervision from the level of the child to that of top policy is a matter of individual concern for the immediately adjacent levels of operating authority, within restricted segments of specialized channels. The criterion for effectiveness is "absence of problems," so that the ideal operation is that which does not involve other than routine approval. Individual initiative, originality, broadening the scope of one's job are matters to be avoided for one's self and to arouse suspicion of motivations when observed in others. Whenever any problem arises, one immediately identifies "responsibility for" the problem, preferably placing this responsibility elsewhere.

With a single exception, the operation of the school at Mopass for Indian children bears a striking resemblance to a well-run stock ranch or dairy farm in which valued animals are carefully nurtured. General health, proper nutrition, shelter, and physical care are efficiently and adequately provided. The children are moved, fed, cared for, and rested by a rotating crew of overseers who condition the herd to respond to sets of signals. Certain individual characteristics and idiosyncracies stand out for the overseer and must be dealt with as they appear, but these phenomena are usually assumed to be inherent in the child without antecedent, to be dealt with by the herder on the spot at his discretion, and to be forgotten when the child is no longer his responsibility.

The single exception is the manner of record-keeping. The system of records that have been kept at Mopass School up to 1962 would be unacceptable in any well-run stock farm, where at the very least, parentage, production records, and performance characteristics of each animal are minimal records to be maintained. Perhaps the most extreme case at the school, but not at all unusual except for the time involved, was the sixteen-year-old girl in the fourth grade who had been at the school for eight years and concerning whom there was not a single word of record beyond the one sheet of number grade scores.

3 / The residential school
as a learning environment

ADULTS OF THE RESIDENTIAL SCHOOL

IN TERMS OF HUMAN INTERACTION, the residential school consists of two worlds: that of adults and that of children. There are varying overlappings, but they constitute separate perceptions of social environment. We shall examine them in operation, first from the adult perspective, then from the child's.

The staff perceives the operation of the school as a replication of conventional home-school relationships. All personnel of the staff, but especially the supervisors, are considered to be parental surrogates; all personnel who teach school classes are expected to function as teachers in model public school situations. This is very explicitly interpreted as not transgressing upon the "parent's" relationship with his children.

The church-employed staff constitute the power structure and the ideological ethos of the school. Their identity, their first loyalty, their source of authority and of status are church-derived; and their primary purpose (aside from self-interest) is the continuity of their church by means of the indoctrination of Indian children in the adult belief system.

The government-employed teachers, more or less professionally trained, are usually members of the same church. Exceptions occur, but Catholics are not found in Protestant schools, nor Protestants in Catholic institutions. Thus, the teachers tend to sympathize with the staff-church interpretations of function. The teachers expect —and are expected—to provide academic skills that will permit the children to progress by the means of normal articulation through regular Canadian schools beyond residential school. Teachers are not expected to become personally involved with the children beyond normal classroom relations.

A defensive atmosphere prevails between the staff—particularly supervisors—and teachers. Staff personnel tend to be poorly educated, even in terms of a general education, and seldom have any specific training relating to work with children. A frequently heard generalization concerns the fact that a lot more than "education" is required to make a good supervisor. (For instance, the following comment: "Why, one of the best supervisors I ever knew could hardly write his name. But the way he could handle those children . . . !") For all their high pay and education, it is believed that the teachers do not know as much about their pupils as do the supervisors, who are with the children in so many different situations. That the supervisors are familiar with the children in a great variety of situations is indisputable, and the teachers go out of their way to indicate their "hands-off" policy and to reassure staff members that the divided responsibility is understood. Teachers operate tight classrooms from 9 to 4, five days a week, and in their off-duty hours lock away all reference to school, classes, and children. As in many small rural schools, the teachers disappear on week ends and holidays and are not to be seen again until 8 A.M. Monday morning. Communication among teachers and staff about pupils tends to be a superficial sharing of cute sayings or humorous misunderstanding anecdotes. Any attempts to speak about purposes, potential, or expectations among either the teachers or the staff invariably lead to plaintive defenses of one's own behavior or to mildly relevant specific case reminiscences.

Staff and teachers alike are generally deviants in the Whiteman society. As agents of cultural change through institutional processes, they constitute a highly unlikely selection if one considers the criteria for such agents to be something identifiable as "representative Canadianness." With the exception of a teacher or two, the adult personnel fit into one of three general categories: (1) relatively recent immigrants from elsewhere in the British Commonwealth; (2) rural Canadians from low socioeconomic backgrounds; (3) Yukon Indians (see staffing pattern, Table 2).

The recent immigrants are of middle or lower middle-class origin and always identify themselves by the country of their birth rather than as Canadian. The nature of their deviance is that, regardless of the degree of similarity among Commonwealth nations, these people are representative of a culture other than Canadian and are themselves foreigners who must cope with some acculturation conflicts in adapting to their new country.

The rural Canadian segment is mostly female. These are people who had "unfortunate" experiences at home—widows who need work to support their children; unmarriageable daughters who eventually become awkward around the house. The pattern is for a friendly local pastor to suggest that residential school work might be "just the thing" and to initiate their applications for work. Few of them are employable anywhere except as domestics. They share a verbalized defensive pride in their nonmiddle-class origin, in their success despite a lack of education, and in their personal experience with "hard work." In spite of these expressed values, the more middle-class immigrant group is the status ideal of the second group. Each of the non-Indians could, and did, trace his own ancestry to identification with one or more European traditional societies.

The Indians were deviant simply in working for the school. Two young girl supervisors were the first such ever to be employed. Others were in low-level domestic positions, but still positions that had usually been held by non-Indians. They quite frankly work for the money. Most of them dislike the way in which the school operates; some, quite verbally so. However, they seldom voice complaints to non-Indians and when they do, it is only in reference to inequities or problems related to their own work.

Salaries tend to be rather good in terms of material return, particularly when compared with the potential earning power of people with similar training and experience in southern Canada. Salaries are also respectable in Indian terms. (A typical wage for adult males is the railroad section-hand scale of $1.53 per hour; waitresses are considered to be well paid at half that amount.)

TABLE 2

STAFFING PATTERN, MOPASS INDIAN RESIDENTIAL SCHOOL, 1962–1963

Position	Sex	Birth-place	Years at Education	Years at Mopass	Maximum Salary for Position
Principal	M	Foreign	13	1	$4500
Vice-principal	M	Foreign	9	4	3500
Secretary	F	Foreign	12	1	2500
*Boys' Supervisor	M	Canada	12	—	2900
Boys' Supervisor	M	Canada	12	1	2900
Boys' Supervisor	F	Canada	8	5	2900
†Girls' Supervisor	F	Foreign	8	5	2900
‡Girls' Supervisor	F	Canada	10	—	2900
§Girls' Supervisor	F	Canada	12	1	2900
Girls' Supervisor	F	Foreign	10	4	2900
Relief Supervisor	F	Foreign	7	—	2900
§Relief Supervisor	F	Canada	12	1	2900
Cook	F	Foreign	8	3	3000
Ass't Cook	F	Canada	8	3	2500
§Scullion	M	Canada	8	4	1200
Dining room supervisor	F	Canada	6	2	2900
§Ass't dining room supervisor	F	Canada	0	1	2000
§Ass't dining room supervisor	F	Canada	10	1	2000
Laundress	F	Canada	8	7	2000
Ass't Laundress	F	Canada	8	1	2000
§Ass't Laundress	F	Canada	13	1	2000
§Janitor (sweeper)	F	Canada	4	1	2000
§Janitor (sweeper)	F	Canada	0	1	2000
Maintenance Man	M	Canada	8	1	3500
*Engineer	M	Foreign	6	4	3500
Engineer	M	Canada	14	—	3500
Nurse	F	Foreign	9	1	3750
*Seamstress	F	Foreign	6	4	2000
§Seamstress	F	Canada	10	—	2000
Night Watchman	M	Canada	8	1	2500
§Relief night watchman	M	Canada	0	1	hourly
Teacher	F	Foreign	16	2	
Teacher	F	Canada	14	1	Range:
Teacher	F	Canada	13	1	4500 to
Teacher	M	Canada	15	1	8000
Teacher	M	Foreign	16 plus	1	

* Dismissed in October.

† Resigned in November.

‡ Dismissed in February.

§ Persons with legal Indian status.

Table 2 shows the twenty-five staff and five teacher positions with data about the incumbents during 1962–1963. Ten positions were held by Indians that year; the previous high had been three. The salaries shown are not those actually paid to any one employee, but are the maximum allowable under the budget. No minimum is fixed, and no set of qualifications exists for any staff position other than that all applications (sent to the Ottawa personnel division of the church) must be accompanied by a recommendation from a local Anglican minister. Principals need not rely upon the Ottawa office for recruitment, so long as they remain within budge allocations and have the Yukon Indian Agency's approval of employees. The former principal had relied exclusively upon Ottawa for replacements; the new principal moved to the other extreme and did not use the Ottawa office at all.

In addition to the base salaries, all non-Indian personnel get an "isolation post allowance" of $480 per year, plus transportation from their home and return to it upon completion of employment. Fringe benefits include medical care; a sliding scale of room and board at the school, with maximum board at $30 per month and rooms from $10 to $30 per month; vacation travel pay for costs in excess of $50 one time per year; and half-fare rail transportation (offered in Canada for employees of charitable institutions, which means the *staff* but not the *teachers*).

Additional benefits for the principal include a house at no charge and full subsistence for himself and his family, drawn from school supplies at a basic charge of $30 per month per adult. He has a choice of being given a car for his own use or having a $500 per year depreciation allowance if he uses his own car. All gasoline and maintenance costs of vehicles are charged to the school.

THE STAFF

In 1962, the four staff non-Indian males (principal, vice-principal, maintenance man, and engineer) constituted the power structure and external image of the school. The principal was a young immigrant with a wife and two children who had almost by accident become involved with residential school administration, after several years of business experience in eastern Canada. One of the few nonordained persons to hold such a position, he soon acquired a reputation as trouble shooter among the schools. The stability that he brought to school administration had already been utilized elsewhere by the church in residential schools rocked by internal dissension. His presence at Mopass was a direct result of the dismissal of the former principal. Other than his obligations as lay reader, he had no regular duties that required his presence. He spent a great deal of time giving personal attention to the school's business in the towns.

The maintenance man's unique position was related to his duty of driving the school vehicle and by his having the complete confidence of the principal, to the extent of being able to operate autonomously. The major uses of the school vehicle were the transportation of local workers to and from school each day and the completion of several round trips to Whitehorse each week. The maintenance man was friendly with most of the people nearby and, in addition to his required duties, did many favors on his trips. (Automobiles are no rarity in the Yukon, but around Mopass, they are still scarce enough so that each trip of any vehicle along the highway is a known event to most residents.) Unmarried and middle-aged, the maintenance man used his school position to enhance his local reputation and to reflect the school positively. He was careful to dissociate himself completely from authority contacts with the children, maintaining a mild joking, avuncular relationship that usually elicited smile responses.

The vice-principal operated within the school almost entirely at a series of personnel tasks in which he experienced considerable frustration. He was a West-Indian Negro who aspired to the ministry and was continuing his studies by correspondence. His real authority was limited to the direction of the Indian help, although under the principal's supervision, he did make schedules for all staff members and children. Staff and children alike ignored him, if possible, and went directly to the principal with their problems. However, the vice-principal was the school disciplinarian and had many interviews with children, occasionally administering punishments, more often using persuasion and counseling. He seldom left the school and never on business. Few people in the towns, whose people knew the principal so well, knew even the vice-principal's name.

The engineer maintained himself, his wife, and their baby daughter almost completely apart from the social life of the school. He had full authority from the principal and a good relationship with the maintenance man, was invariably cheerful and friendly upon greeting, and was seldom involved beyond the greeting stage with anyone other than the various suppliers and service people.

Among themselves, these men maintained a masculine level of discourse in decision-making which excluded the women and children of the school. Collectively, they serve as the impersonal male parent figure: the breadwinner, provider, protector, disciplinarian, and he-who-takes-care-of-the-really-important-things who is so familiar in Whiteman society. (While no Indian was ever taxed with refining the definition of the term Whiteman, the Negro vice-principal found himself in the odd position of being lumped in that category in general Indian perceptions.)

The supervisory staff was dominated by its majority of unmarried middle-aged females who drew upon their traditional concepts of woman's role, church's role, and "proper training for children" to set the tone and pattern of dormitory living. Two young Indian women and one young man were employed as supervisors during the year for varying times, but they did little to change the patterns set by the non-Indian female majority. These three supervisors, along with all female employees of the school, invariably spoke to, and of, one another in formal modes. "Miss," "Mrs.," and "Mr." were required, not only in the presence of the children but even between employees who had known each other intimately for several years. (This contrasted sharply with the practice of the men of the school, all of whom used first names in speaking with or about each other.) The non-Indian women supervisors were spinster ladies of British origin. They had brisk, no-nonsense manners, faintly reminiscent of nurses, and had entered residential school work after varied unsatisfactory experiences with other forms of employment. They referred to themselves as "career people," although none had had more than ten years of formal education. They were active in the church Women's Auxiliary, frequently expressed affection for "their" children and for Indian children generally, as long as they were clean and mannerly. They expressed deep disapproval of the Indian way of life and dismay at the thought that the children they supervised would " . . . probably go back and live just like their parents."

Several supervisors had been dismissed during the early part of the year. One had disliked the children completely, another had disliked the climate, a third had a severe personality disturbance. The supervisory staff stablized when two local Indian women, nineteen and twenty-three years old, respectively, were employed. Both these women had completed the twelfth grade in Whitehorse. They were not only the first Indian supervisors to be employed at Mopass; but they were also the best educated of the school's supervisors. Both were well known to the children of the school, and their coming was received with enthusiasm. One young White male also came to work—his first job of any kind. He and the Indian women were well-intended toward the children, but they were soon told in no uncertain terms just "how things are" by the older women supervisors and conscientiously tried to adapt themselves.

Supervisory tasks are similar no matter who is in the position. A supervisor is constantly on duty and in charge of a given group of children—usually about thirty. So repeatedly that everyone in school is completely familiar with it, the dictum is clearly and explicitly stated that *no one* other than the supervisor in charge is to direct, control, correct, or in any other way interfere with the children unless to provide emergency protection from immediate danger. The four groups of children (senior boys, senior girls, junior boys, junior girls) each have a supervisor continually in charge except while the groups are in classes. Supervisors of junior groups sleep in rooms provided in the children's dormitories; the others have rooms assigned to them on the third floor. A fifth supervisor works relief shifts to provide weekly days off for the other four.

The supervisors wake the children in the morning and see to their washing, dressing, and feeding; their attendance at classes, performance of routine tasks, and recreation periods; and, finally their preparing for bed and getting to sleep. At all times a supervisor is to know where each of his children is and what he is doing. Their duty is constant, five and a half days per week. During school sessions, they relax somewhat but are expected to check clothing, take care of various special cleaning or other dormitory tasks, care for sick children, and so forth. No strict time supervision is exercised over supervisors, and they are free to make informal arrangements for sharing tasks, especially playground and cafeteria supervision.

Throughout all these tasks, the children move, or do not move, at a signal from the supervisor—usually the police whistle, an indispensable part of each supervisor's equipment. No person in the school, including the principal and the senior teacher, diverts a child from a supervisor-directed activity without first obtaining the supervisor's permission. When it is necessary for the principal to correct supervisors (and only the principal can do this), such correction is always done in private conferences. No discussion of policy concerning the handling of the children takes place in the presence of children.

The domestic staff is largely Indian, but dominated by status individuals similar in background to the supervisory staff. The cook, an elderly widow of English origin, thoroughly disliked "colored people" of all sorts—including Indians—and most children because they "are never mannerly." She was inclined to be irascible, and the children disliked kitchen duty. The dining room supervisor, the widow of a French-Canadian farmer, was a favorite of the school children because she often mediated difficult situations between the cook and others. The laundress, a quiet, shy spinster, functioned in a remote corner of the basement and was a sympathetic figure to most of the children. She tended to develop special favorites for no apparent reason and upon them she lavished intense attention and fine gifts. She and her assistants worked regularly, day in and day out, without contacting any children but the few who were invited (with supervisor permission) to partake of her largess in the laundry room. (The children not so favored were casually ambivalent about the situation: mildly envious, but acceptant toward the arbitrary arrangements by which the lucky ones were chosen.) The assistant cook was an organizer and a doer, a volunteer for every activity, in school and outside. She was so eager to dominate that she occasionally alienated adults and children alike in the simple extra activities of the school and church.

Under this group of women, the Indian domestic staff worked. It consisted of a male scullion, a female assistant laundress, a seamstress, two cleaning women, and two female dining room assistants. All but the scullion lived in the nearby settlement and went home each night. While their work was boring and sometimes frustrating, such minor inconveniences could easily be borne in order to obtain the unexpected and welcome additional money. They kept their contacts with the non-Indian staff to a minimum. They were interested in (and of some interest to) the children of the school. All of them had attended that school at one time or another and knew most of the families of the children quite well. But there was never occasion for them to be in contact with the children except for odd intervals when they had short conversations. These were usually about school activities, the child's family, or some event of the near future—simple expressions of interest on the part of children and adults alike, but always terminated at the approach of an adult non-Indian. Such fleeting interactions were of a different nature than their interactions with supervisors and other adults of the staff; some fear was always present that these conversations might be considered "interference."

Indian employees have one general complaint about work at the school which typifies their relationship and status. As a charitable organization, the church-operated school has an option about inclusion of its employees under the government unemployment insurance plan. (The plan involves a small deduction from each employee's paycheck.) Participation by employees of charitable institutions is a matter of total approval; all must be included or none can be. The non-Indian majority of staff employees had voted not to participate and thereby excluded the Indian minority from any chance of participation, even though all of the latter valued such insurance highly. Although this had been explained in detail several times, the recurrent complaint about nonparticipation in the insurance plan was invariably voiced as if the school administration—that is, the principal himself—had made the decision. "I don't know why he won't let us have unemployment. I asked him again, but he won't give it to us."

TEACHERS

The teachers are in the school, but not a part of it. They conduct classes from 9:00 A.M. to 3:30 P.M. and partake in any adult social events according to their inclinations, but do not participate in the other activities of the school, except as a teacher in a public school might be asked to help with a Chritsmas party or a church affair. The senior teacher has classes, organizes other teacher group-meetings, makes reports, and cooperates with the principal through whom all the paper work of the school—whether church or government—must pass. Cordial working relationships between the two require clear and carefully defined spheres of authority. The senior teacher occupies half of a duplex apartment adjacent to the principal's house, the other half being shared by two or three other teachers.

In 1962, the "beginners" teacher had taught at the school the previous year and was regarded as *the* occupant of the duplex building. The new teachers were said to have "moved in with" her. She had been disturbed at finding herself in the preceding year's intense fracas during her first year at the school and was determined to remain aloof from any sort of personal relationship. She performed her duties regularly and conscientiously, politely declining every overture to become involved in other activities, school or social. She responded directly to communications, volunteered nothing, and immediately departed whenever the time was up from both classes and meetings.

The first grade teacher had come from a previous year spent in an Indian day school further south in British Columbia. She said that she had not liked day school teaching and thought that working in a residential school might be more challenging. Her childhood and school years had been spent in a middle-class, suburban British Columbia environment. She drifted into teaching after three years of university training with no real objective other than genteel, premarital experience. College and her previous work had combined to instill in her an understanding that the whole world is not White middle-class, and she was rather surprised to find that she was beginning to realize intrinsic values from the role of teacher. She was interested in her children and her work and spent many extra hours in a variety of activities involving both children and the staff adults.

The second grade teacher had a dozen years of Indian residential school staff experience, but was in her first year as a teacher. From a rural, prairie background, she had begun as a supervisor, then become a seamstress and part-time sewing instructor. A church Women's Auxiliary scholarship from the community in which she then worked had permitted her to attend a college "short course" for a year in order to obtain formal teacher's credentials. She was very proud of her new status and eager—although a little worried—at the prospect of being fully responsible for an entire class in all subjects. She had known the "beginners'" teacher in a previous school and took her cues about social relationships from that teacher. Aside from interactions at church services, she had little social contact outside school hours and no function in the school life other than as teacher.

The third grade teacher was a young Anglo man in his midtwenties, on his first teaching assignment. He was from a middle-class, urban family, having had no prior experience with Indians or rural living. He was stable; traditionally, intensely, and intelligently Anglican; and " . . . not particularly attracted to urban schools." He lived in a third floor room among the staff; was organist for the church services; and conducted himself with dignity, displaying humor and friendship on proper occasions but generally remaining somewhat apart from the staff and other teachers. He created and maintained a role consistent with "teacher" among nonteachers. In the classroom and around the school he worked very hard at getting to know his children and participating in most school activities. Frequently the additional tasks he assumed were in cooperation with the first grade teacher, with whom he enjoyed a pleasant companionship.

All the non-Indian adults of the school shared an attribute that was even more outstanding than their deviance from Canadian culture norms: ignorance about Indians. This ignorance was surpassed only by their willingness to offer snap judgments, usually unfavorable, about basic Indian motivations or character. Not only is there no background of systematic study about Indians or social-change concepts among the residential school personnel, but moreover, their perceptual ranges like those of the fabled blind men and the elephant, are so limited to the immediate environment that each tends to arrive at self-sustaining generalizations which determine daily activities from the daily activities themselves. An occasional exception only accentuates the general pattern and offers glimpses of backgrounds. One teacher, arriving slowly but progressively at some genuine insights, once mentioned that until that year:

> Indians never seemed like people—not *individuals,* I mean. I used to wonder about them sometimes. We'd see them often—maybe a drunken Indian asleep in the back of a bus—and you'd think, "Oh, Indian," like you think lamppost, or tree, or dog. Even last year when I was at (*X*) school, those people were vegetables! I never could get near them. But here; these people are different. They are fun to know. . . .

ADULT RELATIONSHIPS

The important (to them) relationships among the adult population of the school do not directly involve children, yet are frequently observed and interpreted by children. No efforts are made to explain these often fascinating interactions to the children among whom every facet of observed adult behavior becomes quickly shared.

A high degree of tension prevails among the adults in the school. Conflict is pervasive; mechanisms for conflict resolution are at best meager, with inhibition, repression, and extreme anxiety observable in most situations. This was not unique to the 1962–1963 school year. Conflict had been even more intense during the immediately preceding years and finally resulted in the removal of the principal and four teachers from the school.

At the beginning of the 1962 school year, a general attitude seemed to prevail among both the staff and teachers that the preceding unpleasantness had been ended with the replacement of key personnel and that things would be all right now. This proved to be a tentative attitude; the pressures inherent in the situation were unchanged, and most of the personnel were unchanged. As personality needs remain essentially the same from year to year, tensions rapidly mounted under the new principal. They took different channels, but were the same types of conflict: conflicts based largely upon resentment against authoritarian controls; upon each one's perceptions of his own shortcomings, which consequently required ego-defensive measures; and conflicts stemming from unfulfilled personal gratifications for which different people sought various vicarious fulfillments.

Most personnel who remained at the school in 1962 appeared to feel a need to mention the previous year's pressures to newcomers and a simultaneous need for dissociating themselves from an active role in the situation. All members seemed to agree that the essential conflict had been between the senior teacher and the principal and had resulted in lack of cooperation and poorly defined or nonrespected spheres of authority. The one remaining teacher expressed an opinion that the senior teacher's position had been basically right (all teachers except her had emphatically aligned themselves against the principal), but she deplored the writing of letters of complaint to higher authorities, as the teachers had done. She had also objected to the techniques of quizzing the children about staff practices and being critical of the staff in the presence of the children. Her version of the "real" difficulty was plausible (as an immediate, overt situation) and public.

The principal had ordered new furniture, and the 1961–1962 senior teacher was under the impression that it had been authorized for her quarters. When the furniture arrived, the principal not only put the new furniture in the staff lounge, but even had some of the old staff lounge furniture put into the senior teacher's quarters in exchange for some of her original furniture, which he thought would fit the lounge decor more appropriately. From that time, the informant teacher said, communications between teachers and staff practically ceased as the senior teacher led a campaign of criticism and harrassment, at first about school procedures in general, but climaxing in a series of documented charges of personal misbehavior by the principal which were extremely bitter and did not become public.

Staff accounts were not quite so specific, but did agree that a sudden change had overcome the relationship between the senior teacher and the principal in midyear and that communication between them had all but stopped. Staff attitudes toward the former principal ranged from guarded neutrality (he *had* been an ordained minister) to outright approval. "He was strict, but he loved those children . . ." "He was a *good* man . . . " "He had discipline around here! It almost broke his heart when he was dismissed . . ."

The man had been a bachelor, was about forty years old and tall and esthetic in appearance. He was called Father by the female members of the staff (a practice permissible, but not common, in reference to Anglican ministers). Various forms of personal attachment had led to internal conflicts among his supporters, who were predominantly the unmarried middle-aged female staff group. There had been special foods and other favors that "Father liked . . . ", gifts at many different occasions both to and from "Father"; and even a certain competition in making cash donations to the church fund (through "Father" and in his control), which were not kept secret by any means. Triumph in this *sub-rosa* cultivation of the principal's favor had come whenever "Father" showed personal appreciation to one or another of the staff females or made public reference to his appreciation.

"Father's moods" had been the tenor of the school. It was told that, on days when he would enter the children's dining room and stamp his foot for complete silence, or when he would come to the kitchen and thoughtfully stroke the cat with his carefully gloved hands, the staff would know that "something was bothering Father" and they would bustle more than usual in an attempt to find out what was wrong and to do something that would especially please him.

The brisk Scotsman who replaced Father had no stomach for the sort of staff relationships about which he so promptly heard a great deal. He had his own wife and family as a source of primary identification and his own notions of "friendship" in working relations. Casting aside the intimacy and probing into actual work performance, he soon discovered many felt inequities among the staff, at least some of which were quite real. He carefully defined each job in terms of expectations, limits of duties, hours, responsibilities, and assistance. He provided additional personnel and brought salaries into a logical hierarchical scale. At a general meeting early in the year, he said that his purpose was to have everybody know his own and one another's job so that all things would be done by the proper people with no overlapping. He made a special plea for free and public communication about all problems.

His forthright manner was well received by the staff. Even those who missed "Father" most, approved of the clear work definitions. For the first few weeks school functioned quite smoothly as operational parameters were tested and verified. But it was a suspicious group, accustomed to a whole set of implicit assumptions and covert rewards that were now totally invalidated by a mentally healthy, nonmystic principal. His staff was, in effect, anticipating having its individual or collective "feelings" hurt, and it did not have to wait long.

Two persons were so inept as to warrant immediate dismissal. In spite of the principal's efforts to effect resignations or transfers rather than outright dismissals, the staff correctly discerned his intent. Two other dismissals for unacceptable behavior made a total of four staff members (five, counting the wife of one employee) who were victims of attrition and replacement before November. Discontented mutterings and worried conjectures began to be heard. "He's going to get rid of everyone Father liked and everything Father did!" "It's all so different . . . there's no organization, no discipline any more. . . . " Personnel shifts became a major topic of conversation among the staff.

The resignation of the senior girls' supervisor late in November was a climax to the initial period of suspicion development. From then on, a growing fear among the staff affected future relationships. The resignation had come about quite innocently. The principal's wife, in her role as secretary, had been gathering data from staff members for inclusion in a church bulletin that published biographical sketches of all personnel. When the senior girls' supervisor had told the secretary of her several years' experience at Mopass, the secretary commented, "My, that's quite a while. It's about time you'll be moving along somewhere else, I suppose?" She later said that the remark had been a "passing comment," based only on her prior knowledge of staff personnel tendencies to move from school to school within five or so years. However, the supervisor interpreted the comment as a message from the principal through his wife. Despite repeated assurances from both the principal and his wife that any message was unintended and a public invitation that she reconsider, the supervisor resigned and left within a month.

The principal had instituted a Sunday evening open house at his home, which was well attended until November. In spite of the "no shop talk" rule and the fact that few people had anything other than shop talk available, a rather stilted effort was made to dress up and get to the open house each week. The last open house was in the form of a farewell to the departing senior girls' supervisor. From then on, the lines were drawn. Open house was discontinued "until after Christmas" and never again re-established. This was not the end of personal relationships; it was the end of even a pretense of the group unity the new principal had attempted to substitute for the individual relationships that had prevailed under Father.

Many other crises arose which emphasized the schismatic factionalism among personnel. Even the school cat became a focal point in one major episode. The cat often slept in the kitchen-laundry area and, on occasion, used the tunnel connecting the laundry and boiler room as an evacuation area when the nights were cold or she could not get out. The new engineer had made one of his first tasks the transformation of that tunnel from a dark, dirty place to a well-lit, freshly painted walkway. He voiced several complaints to the kitchen crew about cat mess in the tunnel in the mornings. Finally, one day when the principal happened to be in the laundry area, the engineer found more cat sign and let forth with a real blast: "I'm gonna kill that goddam cat if she don't quit crapping in the tunnel!"

It was a hollow threat; the mild-mannered young engineer was perhaps the most unlikely felicide candidate in the school. The principal laughingly agreed with the engineer that, "We'll have to do something about taking care of her. . . . " Later in the day the principal instructed the maintenance man to make a sand box for the tunnel—his interpretation of " . . . taking care of . . . " the cat.

But the exchange had been in the presence of some of the kitchen-laundry staff and it became the basis of a two-week turmoil: "The Incident of the Plot to Kill Father's Cat!" Tears were shed; hot packs, compresses, and pills were administered; plans were made and discarded for various methods of smuggling the cat out or hiding her away. Letters of protest were framed and discarded, and eventually utter resignation prevailed. "They just won't be happy until they've gotten rid of everything Father loved!"

Over the objections of the principal who, along with the engineer, was totally bewildered about the whole incident, one of the most aggrieved participants finally took the cat herself to the Whitehorse Humane Society for disposal.

Such events, verging on the ridiculous when viewed out of context, assume great significance in the total school operation as they become determinants of who *can* speak and who *will* speak to whom. Extraneous events, unrelated or incidental to the welfare of the school children, become salient in staff conversations and activities. Children are cared for by the routine; the major staff efforts are directed toward coping with the intricate complexities of interpersonal adult relationships. No child at Mopass was the object of such deep concern as was that cat.

The principal found it increasingly necessary to have dyadic or small group meetings with various contending persons. His original intention of promoting communication by holding frequent staff meetings, sharing experiences, and so forth, was abandoned. After his initial meeting of the total group during the first week of school, no further group meetings were held during the year.

Staff factionalism had its counterpart sets of relationships among the teachers. A particularly bitter episode climaxed with one of the teachers moving out of the duplex and into the third floor staff quarters. The climax was only a partial solution to a long and continuing disagreement among the teachers and their chronic inability to view situational requirements in the same frame of reference. Two of the teachers were traditional: they adhered to a strict routine and to sets of rules for the behavior of children to the end that days became a totally predictable lock step in their classes. Two other teachers were overly permissive in trying to encourage diverse activities and self-expression; moreover they applied minimum restriction. The fifth teacher hovered between the two stances; he tended to practice in a traditional manner, but continually attempted to relax controls and to instill self-direction among his children. In group discussions among the teachers, the two traditionalists seldom offered comments unless as answers to direct questions. They usually sat with slightly forced smiles while the two permissive teachers did most of the talking and the ambivalent teacher made wryly humorous comments. Such communication became increasingly strained as the traditionalists felt an implied criticism of their classroom operation in the decisions and value judgments expressed by the others.

In addition, the traditionalists were those who had determined that the best staff relationships were no staff relationships, while the other teachers tended to work more or less closely with at least some of the staff in several extracurricular activities and to maintain semijoking, if somewhat distant, relationships with most staff personnel. This further widened the breach between the two teacher factions. It was seldom that the five as a group even approached the broad topic of the purposes and strategies of Indian education. Their group discussions had to do with supplies, schedules, discipline and forms to be completed—and little else.

When the principal employed two Indian women as supervisors in midyear, he thought he saw an opportunity to break the pattern of intense factionalism. He predicted that the Indian women would identify more closely with the children and the children's problems and would thus have less need to draw personal support from the artificial inflation of intrafactional relationships. He was correct; so correct that his action produced an unexpected and hitherto unknown set of conflicts. While the Indian women were effective as supervisors of children, they fitted neither the usual adult, unmarried female pattern of school non-Indians nor the stereotypes those non-Indians had created for Indian adult females. At first, school supervisory personnel attempted to mold the Indian women into their own patterns. When that failed, the Indians were progressively rejected until they quit.

Both the Indian women were young, unmarried, attractive, intelligent, and popular within the total community. They bubbled with energy, chafed with their children at the restrictions imposed by the routine, and introduced little variations to help the children through chores or long empty time periods. On their days off, the new young women supervisors had dates for dances and movies—something outside even the memory of the non-Indian staff, and a very suspect experience indeed. The

Indian women supervisors were occasionally lax in maintaining the children within lock-step bounds and, perhaps worst of all in the eyes of the non-Indians, could often explain deviant child behavior in rational terms. The old supervisors and staff members tended to know children as stereotypes; within a few weeks of each child's entry into Mopass School, he is by general agreement labeled as "good" or "a bad one," "promising" or "unpromising," an "honest one" or a "liar." Such labels tend to become self-fulfilling prophecies.

When the young Indian relief supervisor told one older supervisor that a boy identified as a "bad liar" had not told the facts correctly only because he was afraid of being hit but that this did not make the boy "bad," she committed the unforgivable sin of being not only correct, but also more Christian in her attitude than the supervisor who had called the child bad. Not long after that incident, one of the older non-Indian supervisors charged a senior girl under the care of an Indian woman supervisor with stealing a comb. When the charge was denied, the non-Indian supervisor began to slap the girl about the head and shoulders. The Indian woman said, "Stop that!" but the non-Indian supervisor was enraged and did not stop. Accounts of what followed varied, according to informants. The non-Indian supervisor was either "slugged," "socked," "pushed," or "hit"; one way or another, she was suddenly horizontal on the floor, weeping in frustration or pain from the force applied by the Indian woman. Once again, the Indian woman was "right" in that the girl being slapped had been under *her* charge, not that of the non-Indian supervisor; and school rules are absolute about noninterference with children under the charge of another staff member. The principal had to be involved; he supported the Indian woman and chastised the non-Indian supervisor.

But being in the right was not sufficient—nor was being effective in one's work, nor being liked by the children and Indian adults in general, nor a person's wanting to improve her own and others' operational efficiency through study and discussion. All these attributes were displayed by the Indian women supervisors; at least one of them for a while would have seriously considered further formal training for such work. But there are myriad little ways in which rejection can be communicated when close contact is enforced. Most of these techniques were utilized by a substantial number of the non-Indian staff toward the Indian women. The latter were pointedly excluded in so many ways that they finally come to realize that no hope for inclusion existed. Mistakes were criticized, good performance was accepted without comment. Non-Indians would occupy all the seats at a given table in the dining room, leaving only Indians sitting at the other table. Comments made by Indians within a group would fall upon a flat silence, to be broken with irrelevant remarks about other subjects. After six months, the relief supervisor simply submitted her resignation and left within the week. The other Indian supervisor stuck it out for a few more months before finally leaving. Just before her departure, she wrote briefly of how she felt:

> These people here have finally succeeded in driving me around the bend. They are all the same and they make life so miserable for us [Indians] and themselves. . . . Mrs. *X* has been telling all kinds of lies and gossip that made her sick and she had to be put to bed for a few days. . . . I pity these poor little children who have to grow up in such horrible atmosphere, where these people are supposed to be teach-

ing them how to live and they don't know the first thing about it. I'll be a real coward, but I've never in my life had to put up with such things before in my life so why should I start now. I just feel that I'm fighting a losing battle and I want to get out before my head does. . . .

CHILD RELATIONSHIPS

Although there is virtually no time during a child's life at residential school when he is not under the observation of an adult and in general behaving in accordance with norms established for the situation by adults, there are many child behaviors in which no adult is immediately involved. These behaviors constitute the child's life patterns within the school; from that base are incorporated his perceptions and the results of his interactions with adults as well as with other children.

Two patterns in child relationships become apparent upon even short observation. The first is that Indian children are almost never alone and that their selection of companions is highly significant. The second is that female children in the school are dominant and domineering in comparison with male children.

Not being alone is more than simply being a member of a group. Within groups, each child always has a friend or friends with whom he is physically near and has frequent touching contact. The pair or small group (almost never more than three) constitutes a special entity within the larger group. These special relationships most frequently derive from antecedents to school experience. They occasionally are matters of blood relationships, but such relationships do not necessarily lead to a primary friendship relation. Several sibling pairs in the school are so casual in their relationships as to defy identification as relatives from observation of the siblings behavior. Yet each in these pairs maintained his own close contacts with special friends. Family status is one important determinant in selection of friends. Some families never mingle on a close friendship basis and invariably express distaste toward one another; other families invariably command respect behavior from all the others toward all their members. These instances are beyond the powers of the children to explain, but the feelings are firmly embedded. Some of them are continuations of family feuds known to adult members of the families; others are unknown in origin even among adults. (They may be persistences from long-discarded and all but forgotten social structures in which different status relationships had existed.) In school, the origin of the attitudes is not so important as is the fact that they exist and operate to determine patterns of association that are largely unknown to the non-Indian operators of the school.

Age grade is another important element in friendship formation among children of the school. A child is more likely to select as his best friend, someone of his own age from a friendly family rather than someone from his own family but two or three years younger or older. However, a strong set of supportive, reciprocal obligations exists between older and younger siblings. In times of trouble, their support is assumed and forthcoming. A younger child unfairly treated by another will immediately threaten to get his big brother or sister. Either of the latter, if approached by the younger, will see to vengeance. Much childish teasing goes on, as it does among any group of children. Occasionally the teasing reaches an intolerable point at which threats become necessary. A threat that carries great weight is, "You better watch out that stuff. I gon beat up your little sister [brother]!" This is much more effective, where possible, than threatening to get an older sibling for support. In fact, the threat to harm a younger sibling always terminates the teasing, since it elicits extreme agitation. It usually ends interaction altogether, unless it results in more serious counterthreat or open aggression. Such remarks are made only between real enemies; no chance of friendship exists between people who speak such threats to each other. The enmity is affirmed even if no overt consequences follow the verbal exchanges.

Friendship involves much physical contact. Friends often touch each other, holding hands, entwining arms, patting, or sitting together so closely as to be in contact. There is no difference between male and female behavior in this respect, although the two sexes do not often intermingle. Boys hold hands or walk together with their arms around each other as casually as do girls. Such contacts are strictly limited to friends. Being touched, even accidentally, by a nonfriend is stimulus for immediate touch-retaliation with results varying from hostile standoff to a full-scale battle.

Female dominance is more than physical size, although girls *are* taller and heavier than boys of the same ages. Among girls at the Mopass School there is a greater total volume of conversation than among boys. That is, more words are spoken and conversation is more apt to be volunteered; in comparison with boys, girls tend to speak relatively complete sentences and they do their speaking with more assurance. In addition, girls play more actively, range farther around the premises, and engage in more varied and imaginative play. Girls are the best students and at the same time the worst behavior problems, since they explore more deviant avenues of behavior. In any mixed group activity, success or failure depends more upon the attitudes of the girls than upon those of the boys.

This dominance may well reflect the more secure and better defined set of role behaviors available to girls than to boys in the school. From the traditional Indian matrilineal descent patterns as well as from their high value as economic partners comes an initial impulse toward female importance both as "carrier of the line" and as "keeper of the home." From government welfare-legislation and policy interpretations comes reinforcement of female importance. Women are almost always the recipients of whatever government welfare money comes to the family and are considered by all social workers as the key persons in the family even though the government has legislated changes in descent and naming. From the non-Indian society with whom Indians have the most contact (the transient population) comes added bias about the importance of women, who can always count on being considered social assets if they are willing to become sex partners. Finally, the traditional non-Indian church staff continually upholds ideals of "ladies and gentlemen," in which ladies receive certain preferential treatment. All these factors tend to affirm female importance and female security, while they at the same time deny any equivalence to the male and fail to provide alternative male role behaviors. In short, it is theoretically easier for an Indian girl child to see a secure set of role behaviors for herself in a Whiteman-dominated society than it is for a boy child. To say that this is responsible for the more aggressive behavior on the part of girl children is purely hypothetical, but it seems reasonable that at least some of these factors are responsible for such behavior.

Children's play activities at the school are usually nondirected. Time in playrooms or on the playground is free for whatever activities the children choose, except for a very few periods when baseball or hockey are required. The free play is very aggressive among both sexes—considerably more so than would be expected among non-Indian children. Some efforts at teaching children's games have resulted in knowledge of various ball, tag, and circle games. Most of these involve rules too complex and do not accommodate the needs of Indian children; they are never played as learned, but are adapted to meet the felt needs. A primary need of each child is individual victory, preferably for himself. If this cannot be achieved, victory for his best friend is next best and victory among his friendship group is a good, but lesser, satisfaction. Gratification of that need is best expressed in non-Indian terms as one-up-manship. In its simplest form, the victory may be stated as being a result of individual *A*'s touching individual *B* in such a manner that *B* cannot retaliate. *A* wins. If *B* manages to retaliate, he not only negates *A*'s victory, but he himself then becomes victorious. If, for physical contact, there is substituted *all* observable interaction—talking, touching, looking, recognition by others, indeed the total human environment—as a direct reflection of personal status, it is possible to perceive something of the complexity of relationships among Indian children. To the objective viewer, the play of children is a chaotic period of frenetic activity coming to a climax with both weepings and exclamations of triumph, followed by a relatively quiet planning session for the next frenetic activity. Within this context, most group games that stress sportsmanship and coordinated activity without personal victory are meaningless; they are rejected by the children of Mopass School.

A common phenomenon that illustrates a form of aggressive interaction other than verbal or physical contact, and that invariably puzzles non-Indians who attempt to settle disputes, is the aggrieved complaint that "He popped his eyes at me!" as a basis for overt aggression. This is recognized by the children as justification for socking somebody. It means the aggressor has opened his eyes wider than usual and stared directly at the injured party. No implication of power being involved in eye-popping is heard; it appears to be more on the order of an unstated inference that the person so looked at was "funny"—that is deviant, queer, abnormal.

Children's conversation among themselves is sparse—a semipidgin jargon they bring from home, supplemented by gradually expanding patterns picked up at school but still tending toward nonsentence utterances of basic noun-verb combinations or even a monosyllabic noun or verb expressing sentence meaning by varied inflection. Swearing in Anglo terms is outside the language corpus of the children, but some English words have been adapted from church-school use to have very unsavory connotations when used among children of the school (and among Indians outside school, also). Commonest of these words are "funny," "dirty," and "stupid," any one of which is insult supreme. (The unwary teacher who uses these terms is doomed to ineffectiveness!) The insult potential of this class of word is contained in nonverbal meanings pervasive among the Indian population. "Funny" has the connotation of "queer" in one common English usage among Whitemen, but the implication among Indians is that the "funny" person is so queer or deviant as to be an object of personal ridicule. "Dirty" and "stupid" have been commonly used derogatory terms among non-Indians since contact times, so much so that the rather mild connotations of the terms as used by Whitemen are incomprehensible to Indians and, in turn, the terms currently have meanings among Indians that are all but incomprehensible to Whitemen. The intensity of their meaning is illustrated by the fact that adult Indians have fist fights and even break up homes over the use of those words.

A great deal of letter writing takes place among the residential school children, as it does beyond the boundaries of the school also. Letters are written to family and friends away from school; to siblings and friends at the Whitehorse hostel; and, most frequently, to friends within the school itself. An unverified, but not unlikely, hypothesis is that more actual words of communication are exchanged among the children by means of letter than are orally exchanged at the school. Most children write one or more letters each day if they can get the paper; many children write many letters. First grade children just beginning to create single words frame them into letters as soon as possible. Letter-writing ability is a first objective for the students. A prideful transition point in one's life is reached upon delivery of one's first letter to a friend.

The content of the letters is stilted and rigidly patterned. It is relatively unimportant; the *act* of sending a letter is an expression and affirmation of the reciprocal bonds of friendship. Almost everything in the letter is predictable except the addressee and certain names mentioned in the text which are significant indicators of shifting or nonshifting alliances. The near-invariable pattern of writing is to begin with an offhand, casual comment: "I just thought of writing to you. . . ." or "Well, here I am with nothing to do and I will write. . . ." Next in order is a query and a statement about well-being: "How are you doing [getting along] at your [place]? I am doing fine at [my place]." Third in order is the friendship reference in which names of friends are mentioned (but *not* attributes and seldom actions): "My best friend here is [name]." "My other friends are. . . . Who are your friends? . . . I have many friends at this place. . . ." Very rarely, among older children, opposite sex members will be named. Seldom is there added information in the letters and any that is included is in the nature of an afterthought comment about a salient activity. Grand decorations, usually with a religious motif; margins filled with flowers; and crosses and friends' names adorn each letter. The letters control, direct, and effect continual power shifts among the various friendship groups of the older students (second grade and upward), but their stylized format is unchanging.

The letters seem patterned after adult letters. Even in writing to officialdom, letter after letter from Indian adults in the agency files follows a similar pattern: "Dear Sir, I just thought of writing to you. How are you getting along at Whitehorse? We are fine at this place but got no food. Please send us a fish net and 30–30 shells. My friend Charlie could use some too. Yours truly. . . ."

The adults of the school have varying policies about letter writing and passing, but they do not really inhibit the traffic. Letter content is so innocuous and stilted as to have small meaning for the adults, who perhaps deplore the "wasted time" but generally abandon any real attempt to rechannel the efforts put into letter writing. A similar attitude prevails among adults toward the many other child behaviors that do not appear to have any importance to the over-all function of the groups.

COPING WITH ADULTS

A child's first learning task at the residential school is to perceive the limits of permissible behavior for each environment and with each adult. Environmental behavior norms are relatively simple. The several variables—playroom, dormitory, chapel, classroom, and so on—are clearly defined. Adults have set the limits and passed the word; basic socialization simply through being with the group for a week or so suffices to impart general understandings about dress and manner. More difficult is the task of each child to adapt himself to the personal idiosyncrasies of the various adults who are important in his life. To be successful, each child must sharpen his perceptive powers, observe closely, and test carefully when approaching boundaries to see that he remains within limits.

Mopass children must view the adults as controllers of fate. God may have His uses; but it is the supervisor who allows one to attend the movies, distributes new clothing, and cuffs the backside of him whose hair is improperly cared for. Thus, while adults are seldom interested in analyzing individual children, the children are intensely interested in the analysis of every bit of observable adult behavior. The children of the school are thoroughly pragmatic; are able to shift behavior patterns at the toot of a whistle to adapt to the individuals in charge of them; and throughout this shifting, invest as much of themselves as is demanded by the activity and the supervisor at hand, but no more.

The children are easily directed. They perform readily as long as they understand what is wanted; they prefer that directives be clear and simple. They very much dislike having to make decisions themselves. Almost any adult can command almost any behavior from the children and receive satisfactory response, especially if he has a whistle. When presented with alternatives, however, the children display extreme anxiety and almost demand direction unless he who has presented the alternatives has also clearly indicated his own choice—which will then become the children's choice. It is easy for school adults to interpret this behavior as a cultural or racial characteristic of refusal to commit one's self, unwillingness to undertake autonomous activities, or lack of initiative. To the extent that it is a typical response in Whiteman-Indian relationships, it is a phenomenon of acculturation. The fact that children always wait for directives, even in the most routine situations, is somehow not connected by Whitemen with the fact that these children are never encouraged to make personal decisions or choices among real alternatives. It is taken as prima facie evidence that directives are needed.

"They're only children; even their parents are just like children in so many ways. . . ," is a common theme. "You *have* to *tell* them what is right." Over a period of many days, such directives constitute the totality of verbal communication from most adults to the children. In terms of incoming messages, children get few soft words, gentle inquiries, or personal encouragements. There is only *the word*.

> Now it's time for. . . . *Every*body get in line! Hurry UP, It's time to . . .! All junior boys, MOVE! ALL senior girls, UP the stairs! Hurry . . . Hurry! Be QUIET! Stand UP! Go. . . . Sit down. . . . Come. . . . Do. . . . Don't. . . . Hurry! Hurry! Stop that this INstant! Speak up. . . . Be quiet . . . Hurry . . .

With whistles continually interspersed among the foregoing medley of directives, words spoken in a variety of strange voices, inflections continually rising, and pitches a level or two higher than in normal conversation, the cacophony of sound which daily assails the ears of a child in the residential school is appalling.

A canteen is operated by the vice-principal to provide bits of candy for the children once a week. Several varieties are available. Children who have not lost canteen privileges as punishment for minor rule infractions are lined up on canteen day and they file past the little counter where they select a limited amount of the offered goods. Some families send money; it is kept by the vice-principal, and canteen purchases are charged against the fund. Those with no money get an allowance from a church-donated fund. All have the same amount available at canteen and are told what they can have in terms of quantities of candy of each variety, not in money terms. They never handle money. Even the oldest children often do not know the names of coins or how to count change. When the principal was asked why he did not permit children to use money and to function as storekeepers as well as customers, he was shocked at the idea. "Why they'd NEVER be able to handle that. It'd get all mixed up . . . take all night to run 'em through." To the suggestion that the stock be expanded from candy only to little toys, hair ornaments, writing materials, and so forth, he was equally opposed. "They have a hard enough time making up their minds as it is. . . ."

Within this framework of relationships, it is not surprising that direct questions to individual children, or direct invitations to make verbal responses of any kind most frequently result in silence. The one mode of communication that is neither rewarded nor encouraged, is volunteered information of a nonemergency nature. Failure to elicit responses from children often leads to further directive adult behavior which thus further reinforces inhibition of spontaneous verbal responses and, in the end, contributes to the self-fulfilling prophecy analysis.

Every teacher shares initial classroom frustrations at the lack of verbal responses from the residential school children. Children will write on paper, move as directed, and even read from books when told where to begin. They do not respond to questions such as "Who knows the name of that mountain?" "Who is the oldest person in this class?" "Who can tell us . . . ?" "Who would care to suggest . . . ?"

After patient, careful work, some teachers manage to reach a point where oral communications in class is at a rather high level within a restricted range of topics. Venturing beyond the pragmatically tested range of material, or attempting to transfer the growing verbal ability too quickly to other situations, most often meets with complete relapse into nonverbal behavior.

The children's behavior modifications at the school are specific to each adult; these modifications are not general behavior changes. If Teacher X wants a child to comment upon the relevance of facts to a given situation, one comments. That does not mean that Teacher Y or Supervisor Z wants similar comments. The essential learning is that which leads one to discern and to satisfy—if possible—the needs of the power figures who control the learner at the moment.

It may well be that the learnings in such variable situations are essential to rapid acculturation, but that set of learnings is not the rich, personal experience of expanding self-realization which is intended by curriculum policy or by well-meaning teachers.

A hedonistic individualism can be observed in development among the various grade levels of children. "Beginners" enter school in great awe and no little fear. Many have never before seen buildings with three stories, ten steps leading to the entry, and so forth. Few of them know indoor toilet plumbing or kitchen equipment or many of the other artifacts of school life. For their first few months they literally tremble with eagerness to please and to fit into the scheme of things.

Toward the end of the first year, or early in the second, there comes a period of burgeoning confidence and a tentative reaching out for closer identity with the school adults. At those age levels, children occasionally volunteer conversations with adults; enjoy sitting near, or holding hands with, adults; or sharing an activity in which an adult is participating. They *feel* themselves learning; they know that learning is thought of as good; and they seek affirmation of their expanding identity through increased interaction with the power sources. To that point, they move more or less together toward a common goal and they are ripe for acceptance and inculcation with a group ideal.

But acceptance does not come from the adult non-Indians—not the acceptance as a growing, changing individual which the child seeks. Adult criteria for approval are static and based on inconsequential things (to the child) related to the adult's job performance: how straight a line is kept when children walk together, how little talking is done at chapel, how politely a child says, "Excuse me, ma'am," when he walks in front of a lady, how neatly he letters and underlines the date at the head of a page. And these criteria are not related to the things that really matter to the child; the learning he feels as evidence of his own maturation.

Often those children who learn the most rapidly find that they have the most trouble and are accorded the least acceptance, because their rapid learning leads to added leisure that has to be filled with some kind of activity—activity all too seldom provided from anywhere other than the child's own inventive self. Far from meeting with acceptance, such activities lead to punishment as deviant behavior. Punishments are usually more severe than one cares to encounter. Beatings can be endured, but beatings are infrequent. The most frequent punishments are removal of privileges, confinement, or isolation—all of which involve serious damage to one's image with others, as well as to his own ego. It is therefore often necessary for children to lie when discovered in any behavior that was not specifically directed.

Seldom is a confession made when authority seeks to assess the origin of such deviant behavior. It may not be "bad," but if it has not been specified as approved, it is better to have no connection with it at all than to be associated with deviance. This, in turn, often leads to entire dormitory groups being put to bed early, or made to stay in from play period, or made to miss the Saturday movie because "nobody would tell. . . ." While the children respect such silence, most of them know upon whom to place the blame and the individual's identity image is still tarnished. The inconsistency and unpredictable severity of such punishments has the effect of further repressing the children's overtures toward acceptance. (Once the entire boys' dormitory was put to bed immediately after dinner for a month—including movie nights—because they had not remained silent after lights out, and nobody would reveal who had been telling stories in the dark.)

Direct approaches of children toward adults are acceptable to a point, but meet with adult rejection before they reach a point of satisfactory friendship in the children's terms. Whiteman adults (especially maiden ladies) are usually averse to the physical contact that Indian children consider essential to expressions of friendship. Children quickly learn that a gesture which, to them is a caress, to many Whiteman adults is distasteful "pawing." By the time children reach the second grade, most overtures from them toward the adults have vanished and been replaced by silence and a wait-and-see attitude that requires absolute assurance of neutral or positive consequences before behavior occurs. No older student ever volunteers to hold hands with an adult non-Indian or displays eagerness for any event or reward until he is completely sure that the cost is not too great. When completely reassured, he then takes all the reward possible immediately, sometimes gluttonously, until the reward is gone or he is thoroughly sated.

Each reward situation is a totality: when the reward is gone, the next situation has to be approached in the same way all over again, always cautiously. With various adults who manage relatively consistent responses, some degrees of assurance are achieved to the end that similar situations can be approached without enduring the *entire* evaluative routine, but new situations and new adults bring immediate regression to the know-nothing state of take-off.

By the time children are in their third year at school, they simply prefer routine as the simplest way of coping with life. The spark of learning for learning's sake is gone, replaced by a pragmatic gamesmanship. Decisions are detestable events unless one directly benefits from them. It is much better to have adults make any necessary decisions, or to have the decisions made by chance, than to be personally involved. Thus, if the group is on a picnic and has carried a bag of sandwiches along, the teacher or supervisor should distribute the sandwiches. If a child is told to help himself, or if the group is told to take what they want, each takes as many sandwiches as he can hold or as others will permit; and somebody will find himself without, standing in mute acceptance of his fate while immediate neighbors are biting from sandwiches held in each hand. Since the decision on distribution was made by the authority, it is up to the authority to see to anyone who is unfairly treated.

Once, a group of five children was to be chosen from a class to attend a special event in town. All the children wanted to go. The teacher insisted that the class should choose the five. Unanimously, the children said the teacher should make the choices. A total impasse was reached when the teacher suggested voting; the group refused even to discuss a vote. Other alternatives were considered and finally, when two days of trauma had passed and the children discerned the teacher's inflexibility about the decision, they agreed to draw numbers out of a box. Chance is more reliable than voting and losing to chance is more acceptable than losing to an expressed decision of one's peers.

This hedonistic attitude seems directly related to the children's perceptions of the absolute power of Whitemen to control the distribution of rewards. It is specific to the school situation. Although no community analysis was made in this study, the many informal observations of situations where Indians were in control never indicated selfishness, gluttony, or disregard for the welfare of the general group—the elements present in many residential school situations.

Children—at least the older ones—appear to realize the artificiality of the school self that they have to create in order to function. When they are in absolutely secure, nonschool environments, rare moments of seemingly honest insight occur, during which they express surprise at themselves or feel the difference between their behaviors in different environments. Walking along the lake shore late one afternoon, the group straggled in twos and threes as it returned from a long hike. A twelve-year-old girl reminisced about her home and earlier years. The teacher walked along, listening and not speaking. The girl spoke randomly of playing with friends and horses, of berry-picking and hunting trips, of the profusion of flowers near her home. She knew the teacher was to leave when school ended that year and she asked, "Why you go way from here? You no like?" The teacher, in a thoroughly patterned response, repeated her question in correct English and then answered that he liked the school and the people all right, but had other work that required him to leave. The girl then said, "I wish you live some other place with us. Not school. At school we all the time act like babies. At home not like that. We're not babies at home."

Another time, on a long, quiet ride to Whitehorse, a ten-year-old asked from nowhere, "Who are our enemies?" It turned out that she was quite confused about Communists, Russians, Germans, Japanese, Chinese, enemies of God, enemies of the church, nonfriends, and germs that were one's worst enemy. A lengthy discussion ensued, which terminated with her declaration, "I think I will have no enemies except I can see them."

Later, back at school, when the teacher attempted to restimulate conversations on similar topics, the children simply could not participate. It was as if they themselves perceived not only two orders of reality functioning within the school—a non-Indian and an Indian—but even that the Indian reality was rigidly segmented into school Indian and nonschool Indian.

CLASSROOM BEHAVIOR

Children everywhere must learn to cope with variable teacher expectations and the variable personality needs of individual teachers. For Indian residential school children, the classroom is but one more environment in which this type of learning is essential to a comfortable life pattern. Teachers, in residential schools and elsewhere, are seldom aware that such learnings are of an entirely different order than those they seek from the accumulated sets of articulated subject matter which they regularly present to the children.

As a universal aspect of student-teacher relationships, learning *to cope* with situational needs is a prime determinant of the nature of learning outcomes among students. Simply stated, it involves an early decision in the course of any sequence of events, anywhere, when the student determines that he *will* or *will not* participate in the teacher-directed intellectual activity of the moment. If he participates—that is, attends to and becomes involved in the teacher-stimulated activity—he is well on his way to achieving the teacher-desired outcomes. If he decides not to participate, however, he is committed to developing a whole series of evasive strategies in order to cover his nonparticipation. Perfectly conceived and executed evasive strategies, particularly if supported by group effort, can result in both minimum energy output and avoidance of the necessity for involvement with the complexity of teacher needs. Many teachers fail to recognize this strategy as a kind of *learning* that follows the same lawful processes and has the same power as any other learning. When outcomes are inconsistent with teacher objectives, teachers invent terms to identify reasons and to classify "slow learners."

Residential school Indian students have sets of evasive strategies so thoroughly internalized that they are almost conditioned responses. So few teacher behaviors in the children's school experiences have been intrinsically rewarding that the decision *not* to participate is all but a given for each new situation. A majority of residential school children are identified one way or another as "slow learners."

It was earlier mentioned that residential school children are easy to direct and to control. It is equally easy to lose control of the children. Achieving genuine involvement on the part of the children in whatever task is at hand, is difficult. Hence teachers tend to concentrate on physical control, discipline, and discrete learning events, while the children, recognizing a game element in the control situation, concentrate on avoiding control by giving the minimum essential task performance.

The ease of control is a function of repression. An authoritative manner, a set routine, prompt retaliation for deviant behavior, and repeated admonitions about conformity are the usual teacher behaviors in the residential school. Shame, sarcasm, ridicule, and disgrace are the weapons at hand for the teacher, while praise, privilege, or just being left alone are the rewards available to the children. The children are accustomed to being herded into classrooms, seated in rows, read to from books or asked to read from books, and told to write things on paper. As long as they are told exactly what to do and when to do it, and are watched carefully to see that they are doing that and nothing else, they perform the various activities in an orderly fashion. Periodically they regurgitate certain remembered segments of those learning activities to varying degress of teacher satisfaction.

This experience has been so common to children of the residential school that deviation from it can be catastrophic for teachers. Each teacher experiences similar nonresponse situations in his class at the beginning of every school year. The children simply refuse to commit themselves until they have the security of their evaluation of the teacher's expectations. The nonresponse is not simple failure to understand; the children will follow any directions except those directing them to speak or to make decisions between alternatives. Although their language patterns are skewed from usual English, those children who have been at the school for two or more years have a wide experience in comprehension of varieties of spoken English.

The experience they do *not* have is in expressing themselves extemporaneously and in making decisions.

Thus loss of control comes to the unwary, well-meaning teacher. Provision of alternatives most often leads to random responses without any regard for consequences, since the projection of consequences has not been a part of the children's conscious experience. Several teacher experiments with permissive relaxations of prescribed routine led to near chaos that rapidly drove the teachers back to repressive routines. In one case, a primary teacher attempted to adapt to his class the linguistically contrived technique of teaching conversational English which has been developed (very soundly) by the Indian Affairs Branch. The highly unusual experience of "just talking" without having group prescribed pencil-and-paper tasks was so exhilarating that the class dissolved into frightened gabble once they became involved. When the teacher attempted to quiet the group, he was forced to achieve utter silence before being able to recommence and, upon asking individuals to speak one at a time, received no response whatsoever. After several repetitions of the situation, the lesson was abandoned and the plan sat unsued on the shelf. The teacher feared ". . . what people might think if they saw the class behaving that way."

Another teacher developed a plan for his more able students to proceed at their own pace in skill work of arithmetic and reading. When the plan was presented, children readily accepted it without question. They were to do as much of a given sequence of tasks as they were able and as rapidly as they could, being exempted from all routine discussion and assignment and asking questions of the teacher only if they needed further information. Several of the brightest children were obviously capable of doing all the required grade-level work with no further instruction, other than occasional reassurances. When the plan was put into effect, days went by with little or nothing being done. The teacher occasionally checked with these children who never had any questions and who never had any tasks performed. For three weeks this teacher managed to adhere to his promise that the children could proceed at their own rate, without imposing his own will upon them as to what the minimum rate should be. No performance at all resulted, and the teacher felt forced to become directive again since the best students were involved and were doing nothing.

Residential school children in classes enjoy talking and enjoy the feeling of learning, but they require continual support and reassurance that they are, indeed, learning. They do not enjoy talking in formal situations in which attention is focused upon them. Even able students dislike reciting. A group conversation can be initiated among them if the children are allowed to speak in unison or several at a time, in disconnected spurts of utterances (or in more formalized choral speaking). As soon as attempted are made to narrow such discussions down to one speaker, silence and embarrassment prevail. Teacher insistence upon individual responses leads the general tone back to recitation and away from spontaneity. As a result, teachers come to be satisfied with simple, minimal recitations; and a whole set of learnings which would be important to future adaptations in Whiteman schools and society are bypassed. This happens at a time when the usual Whiteman child is learning to manipulate and expand his own unique perceptions of his universe; to test and evaluate himself as an individual of worth in his own society through a variety of individually expressive experiences in his school classes.

The residential school child at this stage is increasingly identifying himself as one of a group and affirming that "learning" must involve directed tasks and books. Teachers (generically, including *all* adult models) are unpredictable and inconsistent; books are predictable, constant; the ability to cope with a book is evidence to one's self and to others that progress is being made. Residential school teachers do little to alter this perception, being ever-mindful that the ultimate effectiveness of their function is to be evaluated by other teachers in terms of the extent to which the Indian children will be able to handle the book-and-writing tasks of the public schools. A high incidence of failure in later years of school can never be attributed to a given teacher, or at least will not have much effect upon that teacher's career. But a reputation for "lack of control" of a class or for having promoted children who are unable to do the tasks in the next set of workbooks can be very damaging to a teacher.

So the classrooms of the residential school become a strange unreal limbo area. Unprepared teachers caught in situations they do not understand—even though they tend to be sympathetic—have little alternative but to create miniature dictatorships that may be benevolent, but comprise closed social systems within which the children must function. The children's behavior with teachers is essentially the same as with supervisors. To this extent, the school "reflects its society."

Teacher communication is very similar to supervisor communication except that teachers do not use the police whistle as a primary attention-getting device. However, they do have handbells, as well as the usual mechanisms of classroom control —rows, seats, monitors, and so forth—that provide consistent control devices.

Occasionally Mopass children are involved in learning genuine control of the intended subject matter. More often, they acquire minimal manipulative skills as peripheral effects while most of their learning is in the nature of exploring strategies for coping with the teacher's control system. The children are not *led* in a regular sequence of learning events; they are *controlled* by task performances that have been prescribed for their grade level.

This partially explains why no records have been kept for children of the school, other than the single final grade each year. That grade indicates the teacher's relative assurance that the child can perform adequately at the next level and, aside from that, the teacher has nothing to say except comments on his control mechanisms. Since these latter are widely variable among teachers, they are not particularly desired by the teachers. Further, from many accounts offered by both the children of the school and the adults of the community, few of the teachers would have been willing to make public the specific repressive techniques they used.

Academic performance in the residential school is perhaps best described as volatile. Unpredictable fluctuations in individual and group performance of skill learning tasks are sources of continual bewilderment to the teachers, regardless of their control techniques. Learnings that seem secure one week will be completely lost the following week. Sudden spurts of enthusiasm among the children will entice a teacher into unguarded optimism, and relaxation of his control mechanisms, which will be followed by dull apathy in academic matters and wild "misbehavior" on the part of children—consequences that leave the teacher more confused than ever.

It is as if the children readily recognize real learning situations as opposed to busy work or control tasks and, when the latter are predominant activities, the total classroom ethos changes from a learning to a game environment. The Indian children are more practiced and more skilled at the game than are their teachers. If any weapon is more effective than passive resistance, it is unpredictability; a combination of the two is unbeatable. Essentially, the phenomena labeled "volatility" are a series of simple, discrete decisions on the part of the children to participate or not to participate in the classroom activities. The teacher is never involved in this decision; is almost never aware of it. The subtlety of this process's operation makes redundant any explicit statement of plan or decision among the children. It is a tragic game in which children win because they are more skilled; and in winning, they lose.

STANDARDIZED TESTS AND THEIR IMPLICATIONS

The ability of Amerind children to achieve adequately as measured by Whiteman tests has been a subject of intensive investigation in various areas over the past thirty years or more. Consistent patterns of performance differences among Indians in comparison with the norms for non-Indian performance have been well established on standardized achievement tests, on "intelligence" tests, and on various personality indexes. (Havighurst 1955). Generally, the "language handicap" and the deviant home environments (considering middle-class non-Indian American as a norm) are considered to be the most important factors in causing the achievement lags and the other differences indicated on such tests. One of the most relevant studies presents extensive evidence of a pervasive, negatively accelerating gap between the median scores of Alaskan Indian children and those of Alaskan non-Indian children on the Stanford Achievement Tests (Ray 1958).

Ray concludes that ". . . the present outlook for academic success on the part of native pupils in a typical school program is not bright. . . ," but suggests that the cultural handicaps ". . . can be overcome through thoughtful instruction . . ." (Ray 1958: 110).

Educational psychologists have developed considerable evidence that the more often a person is tested, the more sophisticated he becomes at handling tests, and that the general effect of test sophistication is an increase in scores, including intelligence quotient scores. (Anastasi 1960: 190–200)

Combining Ray's prescription for thoughtful instruction with the psychological evidence of the value of test sophistication, the study at Mopass Residential School was planned to include a series of standardized tests and the teaching of test sophistication in the fourth grade (which was taught on a full-time basis by the author.) This program was prompted by curiosity as to outcomes and justified by the knowledge that, regardless of cultural background and personality factors, the Indian children's academic futures (and, to a large extent, their *entire* futures) are determined by their performance in traditional schools where test skills are critically important.

With the cooperation of the Regional Superintendent of Schools, two batteries of the Stanford Achievement Test (SAT) were administered. One was given near the beginning of the school year; the second, toward its end. For additional comparative information, the Wechsler Intelligence Scale, Children (WISC) was administered to all fourth grade children at the residential school and to all children, Indian and non-Indian, at a nearby public school. Finally, a climax of the testing, the California Test of Mental Maturity (CTMM) was administered late in the school year. Both the WISC and the CTMM provide verbal and nonverbal component scores and fall in the category of intelligence tests, as opposed to the SAT which is intended as an achievement test. Among users of such tests, it is expected that academic growth will be shown on achievement tests, but that the intelligence tests (yielding results in terms of intelligence quotient) will remain relatively stable over time for the population among whom the tests were standardized.

The teaching of test sophistication was undertaken by providing a regular weekly test as a part of the class routine, except in weeks when one of the group standardized tests was administered. These tests were constructed each week by the teacher and were prepared on duplicated ditto forms of consistent, formal format; they contained items of varying natures but having general similarity to the types of items found in standardized achievement tests. Each week they were checked with achievement tests to be sure that no actual items were included from such tests. On the whole, the weekly tests tended to be more difficult than the achievement tests, as they stressed abilities to draw inferences, to follow relatively complex instructions, and to see relationships. A different arrangement of items was used each week. Test validity was not a specific concern, although the course work of the class was the basis for most of the items included. The principal goal was to provide the children with a wide range of experience in handling a variety of stimulus items in a formal testing contest. No grades were given other than the raw scores on the tests, and no pass or fail mark was set. The results were given each week in terms of class-rank, which was recorded on a cumulative chart maintained on the classroom bulletin board.

A predictable negative response, ranging from moans of dismay to aggressive comments about the "unfairness" of having tests so early in the year, greeted the first of these weekly tests. However, the teacher persisted (authoritatively), and a rigorous test atmosphere quickly came to be an accepted fact to the residential school children who are well conditioned to accepting facts about which they can do nothing. During the one-hour test period nobody spoke or moved from his seat; during the half-hour following the test and before recess, the children were free to pursue their own interests as a reward for their exemplary behavior during the tests. This disciplined activity, followed by the relaxed free period, soon came to be a stimulating experience in itself, with obvious pleasure displayed by a majority of the children.

At the end of the sixth week of school the Stanford Achievement Test, Primary Battery, Form *J*, was administered. Soon afterward, the series of individual WISC interviews were begun and completed within about two months. Eight months after the first Stanford test, the Stanford Achievement Test, Partial Intermediate Battery, Form *J*, was administered; and in the final week of school, the California Test of Mental Maturity, Elementary *S*-Form, 1957, was administered.

A detailed analysis of the test results is presented in the dissertation from which this study is drawn (King 1964). The most striking results of the entire testing procedure are the indications of "normalcy" among the Indian children, measured by means of test instruments devised for non-Indian populations. An achievement gap is clearly evident on both the Stanford tests; but the gain, as reflected both by class means and individual performances, is almost exactly eight months in the age-grade norms established for the tests over the eight-month period that elapsed between the two achievement tests. Individually, the comparable SAT scores show the same variations that can be expected among any population, ranging from little or no gain to almost two age-grade years gain. From these results there seems to be no basis *in terms of academic potential* for predicting that Indian children will not perform as well academically as non-Indian children at a given grade level.

The language handicap under which Indian children operate is clearly discernible in both intelligence tests. The WISC as an individual test, and the CTMM as a group test, both provide separate verbal scores; and in all individual results, as well as in over-all means, the verbal results were lower than the nonverbal. However, the gross scores (combined verbal and nonverbal) of the intelligence tests show no significant differences from what might be expected among a non-Indian group drawn from among the population for whom the tests were standardized. This is a function of the uniformly *above average* performance of the Indian children on the nonverbal components of the tests.

Two reasons can be suggested for the consistently superior nonverbal performance: (1) a high degree of rapport existed between the examiner and the children, directly related to their positive set toward testing as established in the classroom test routines; (2) the language handicap is very real, but all of the rest of the Indian child's experience in residential school tends to make him particularly acute in perceiving and relating to environmental changes. (Further, it is not altogether unlikely that cultural differences exist between Indians and non-Indians, which make the former more perceptive and more able in manipulative skills.)

In a comparison of WISC results of the residential school children with those of the public school children, the few non-Indian children showed a mean intelligence quotient of almost exactly 100 (the normative base score). This lent support to the author's feeling that he had not introduced any systematic bias into the testing, since the same procedures were followed for every child tested. Indian children in the public school show slight tendencies toward the non-Indian test patterns of roughly similar verbal and nonverbal scores; but their performances are still clearly more closely related to "the Indian pattern," as set by the residential school children, than to the Whiteman pattern shown by the non-Indian public school children.

The California Test of Mental Maturity at the end of the school year shows such a remarkable gain that little confidence can be placed in the results. Again, procedures were rigorously followed. Whether the test results can be attributed to a general euphoria that prevails at the close of school, to some unknown skewing influence introduced, or to the inadequacy of the test, it is difficult to say. The last explanation seems the most likely, since analysis of the nonverbal portions of the test shows such superior performance on the part of the Indian residential school children as to make them quite remarkable in comparison with the standardization population if this test were truly valid.

The significance of this teaching of test sophistication and of the testing that was done at Mopass as a part of this study lies chiefly in the evidence it gives that Indian children *can* achieve in Whiteman terms, given some relatively small modifications in the instructional situations and given adequate practice in understanding what is wanted. Most of the achievement and intelligence testing that is reported in the literature of such cross-cultural testing consists of single test events —samples of "reality"—in which the test items, *as test items* and not as items having variable meanings, are assumed to have the same meanings to all the subjects. This is certainly true of the usual standardized test situation in the public schools of both the United States and Canada. Tests are given, seldom more frequently than once a year, on the assumption that the test results indicate variable performance along an individual's single contiuum of ability to deal with the test stimulus items. There is as yet no way to deal with whatever else the tested child may be dealing with as he makes (or does not make) responses to test items.

The Mopass testing offers no further insight into how to deal with such psychological processes, but it does indicate that Indian children are able to achieve for the intrinsic rewards of problem solving, once the pressure factors of the usual test situation are removed. The Mopass children brought to bear upon these tests the necessary dealing with alternatives that is so atypical in their usual life patterns.

The teaching of test sophistication in itself is a limited and artificial objective. However, to the extent that it indicates a potential among the children to transcend a stultifying environment, to perform at a level beyond that "expected" of Indian children, it is illustrative of a latent potential among the Indian people for coping with the acculturation process. When discrete elements of the process which *must* be controlled are made clear and the means of achieving such control are provided, the individuals themselves will take care of building the cultural bridge needed. Often, it seems, the *fact* of cultural differences has been demonstrated and then accepted as an inherent reason for Indian inability to achieve, rather than as an analyzable base line upon which to identify necessary or desirable change elements.

If the teaching of test sophistication does nothing else, it casts considerable doubt upon the expectations widespread among some teachers and researchers, that Indian children are destined to achieve in school at a lower level than non-Indian children. If Ray's suggestion of the need for thoughtful instruction (see "Standardized Tests and Their Implications," this chapter) could be extended to all who instruct Indian children, the level of expectation for the performance of Indian students should merge with the level expected of all children. It is *not* unreasonable to expect a full, normal range of ability or performance from a group of Indian children in school. Such an expectation among teachers could effect considerable change in teacher behavior. Teacher attitudes toward children, their preparation for classes, their conduct of classes, and even their responses to student feedback are all quite different according to whether the teachers are facing a "dull" group, a "normal" class, or a "superior" one. All the evidence at the residential school indicates that the usual expectancy of teachers in past years had been that they were working with dull students.

SUMMARY OF THE SCHOOL AS A LEARNING ENVIRONMENT

For the children, the residential school constitutes a social enclave almost totally insulated from the community within which it functions; yet Mopass School reflects in a microcosmic, but dismayingly faithful manner the social processes of the larger society. Two distinct domains of social interaction exist independently: Whiteman society and Indian society. Where these domains overlap, they do so with common purposes shared at the highest level of abstraction—but with minimal congruence of purposes, values, and perceptions, at the operating levels of interaction. The Whiteman maintains his social order according to his own perceptions of reality. The Indian bears the burden of adaptation to a social order that he may perceive more realistically—and surely he perceives it with a different ordering of reality— than does the Whiteman. From his perceptions, the Indian finds it impossible to accept the social order and, at the same time, impossible to reject it completely. He therefore creates an artificial self to cope with the unique interactive situations.

In the residential school, the Whiteman staff and teachers are the end men of huge bureaucratic organizations (church and national government) that are so organized as to provide no reflection of the local communities. These employees derive their social, economic, and psychological identity from the organizations of which they are members. They validate their identities by effective job performance in organizational terms. The inherent authoritarianism in bureaucracies intensifies as one moves hierarchically downward until at the lowest level one finds maximum reliance upon power sources for authority and minimal local or individual autonomy. Since these employees are the end of the authority chain—there are none below them in the organizational structure to receive transmitted directives—only two outlets are available for reactions to the cumulative authoritarian input. One outlet is the children of the school; the other is interpersonal aggression in seeking closer identification with the nearest source of power.

The criteria for effective job performance are based more on adult relationships than on relationships with the children. The children of the school are little more than components to be manipulated in the course of the day's work. At best, they reflect the employee's ability to control; at worst they are a distractive element to one's psychological equilibrium, which is much more dependent upon relations with other adults. No job at the school is defined in terms of *outcomes,* expected or observable, in the children. As is common in bureaucracies, "Don't rock the boat," is the operating criterion for effective performance. This is literally translated as meaning one should not create or point out problems that upset the routine.

Since all the members of the school adult population are deviant or marginal individuals, both in their total society and within their bureaucracies, their jobs and their social status are precarious. A considerable degree of anxiety about job security prevails; there is a tendency to perceive a threat in any unusual situation or comment. A strong dependency is fostered, which intensifies the need for authoritarianism which, in turn, has been initially responsible for the situation. The net result is continual factionalism with frequently shifting alliances as a result of newly perceived threats from all directions. The goal of the factional alliance is to cement identity with a power source or to protect against those who seem to have closer identification with those sources. The alliances themselves thus become salient realities in the adult school life. Concerns about the consequences of interactions among school adults often assume dimensions so far removed from any Indian School purposes as to seem ridiculous, were they not so tragically effective in dissipating energies that could be directed toward the education of children.

An ideal among the non-Indian adults of the school (which is completely incomprehensible to Indians) is the modified martyr syndrome. *Seeking* martyrdom as an overt behavior is a far different order of behavior and personality organization than *enduring* martyrdom. The seeker often has surrendered himself to a situation in which higher status is unobtainable through the usual channels, yet he is driven by a need for such status. His loss of autonomy and lack of real purpose in life creates intense inner concerns about self-justification, much of which can be somewhat smoothed out if public identification as a near-martyr can be achieved without one's having to endure actual martyrdom. To achieve such identification, one must suffer publicly; not *too* much suffering, but preferably a controllable, constant amount and in a manner that can be shared and observed. The martyrdom-seeker is a difficult person with whom to work or live, since he is forced to reconstruct all reality to fit the self-justifying fantasy role that has developed in his imagination. He is often identifiable as the person who states that his purpose is ". . . to help people *less fortunate than myself . . .*" or ". . . to show them how to live a better life . . . ," rather than making a frank acknowledgment that he is involved in work at which he feels he can achieve maximum personal gratification. None of the non-Indian personnel of the residential school was willing or able to admit that the job he had was the best job he could hope to get, carrying with it more physical comfort and higher status than anything he had previously known.

Children find the adult society of the school impenetrable, although they are at first inclined to be attracted toward it. A special order is developed among the Indian children, based on patterns brought from home experiences and the necessary adaptations they must make at school. Friendship associations, the few free activity choices permitted, and the children's communication system all reflect the Indian adult society of the total community in its adaptation to the Whiteman adult society.

The school children become uniquely adept at personality analysis, since their major task is to cope with the demands of shifting adult personalities. But this analysis is limited to their needs as the children pragmatically perceive them in specific situations. The children have no understanding of the concepts of martyrdom, for example. Much less do they understand why these seemingly well-paid, comfortably housed adults have such complex emotional problems among themselves. To maintain an equilibrium within their own peer group and in their relations with the impersonal adult society, the Indian children adopt the mechanism of creating a school self that functions only within the school boundaries. If this artificial self is not consciously developed, it is at least partially recognized and consciously controlled. The children sustain themselves with the conviction that their "real self" is not this person in the school at all.

Thus, long before the end of experiences at the residential school, the fundamental barriers between Whiteman and Indian are firmly developed, not so much by a conscious rejection on the part of the Whiteman as by a conscious rejection on the part of the Indian child. The sterile shallowness of the adult model presented by the school Whitemen serves only to enhance—and probably to romanticise—memories of attachments in the child's primary family group, and to affirm a conviction prevalent among the present adult Indian generation that Indians must strive to maintain an identity separate from Whitemen (see "Matt Mathews' Family: Yukon Territory, 189- -1962," Chapter 1).

An inevitable conclusion is that the organized purveyors of Christianity bear the brunt of responsibility for the nonfunctional adaptation of Indians in today's Yukon society. This conclusion is not an indictment of any church, or of the good and conscientious people who have made contributions by way of church responsibilities. It is, rather an assertion that Canadian society has forced upon the churches collectively, both by default and by actual direction, a function that the churches are incapable of performing. In a sense, the Christian churches have been the Whiteman's scapegoat—the buffer instruments with which he hoped to assuage his collective guilt and polish his tarnished conscience.

Christianity was "given" to the Indian by means of the churches and church schools, as a primary acculturative pathway. In all of the contact period and down to the present time, churches were the chosen instruments for "dealing with" Indians. To Indians, church people were the Whitemen most genuinely interested in them; and church people appeared to have a status in Whiteman society that guaranteed acceptance in that society if one identified with the Whiteman's church. Yukon Indians accepted Christianity so wholeheartedly that, within two generations, they had abandoned basic cultural patterns in a matter seldom before known to anthropological science. Language, technology, and custom became archaic overnight. Their very name identities and attendant patterns of ceremony and tradition were totally abandoned in favor of Christian identification.

Unfortunately, their newly acquired morality concepts proved to be unrelated to political and economic power in the Whiteman's society; or, at least, related in a manner not clear to Indians. Christian morality is not a set of precepts by which White businessmen do business or White workingmen labor or White social leaders accumulate prestige and wealth. Christian morality is the Whiteman's symbolization of a set of ideals which *he* recognizes as unattainable, but which he supports by means of an institutionalized social appendix called a church because this set of ideals acts as a source of forgiveness which compensates for the complexity of his individual rationalizations of self-interest and his acquisitive motivations. The subtle complexities of guilt-sin-forgiveness-salvation which have been developing among Whitemen for nearly two thousand years have not been easily transferable to Indians within only a few generations.

The Whiteman was—and is—willing to give his idealized moral order to the Indian. Indeed, he is quite insistent about it! He was not—and he is not—willing to give political and economic power to *anyone* if he can keep it for himself. To the Indian, whose indigenous individualistic morality was very similar to that of the Whiteman's—minus the superimposed Christian ideals—the new morality introduced by the Whiteman seemed a wonderful protective device for the stabilization of society, representing a great advancement for man. But the disillusion of finding that the "new morality" was only verbalization, and not a set of functioning precepts for living, has proved bewildering and disintegrative. Indian attitudes have shifted from eagerness to be a part of that society to eagerness to get what one can *from* that society.

Such an attitude is reinforced by the would-be martyrs who come with a missionary zeal. Whereas the true missionary is seldom concerned with direct self-gratification, the deviant, misplaced "missionaries" feel themselves to be self-sacrificing bearers of truth and light to a shadowed place of sinful error. This becomes an essential motivation and a broad justification for such inadequate individuals, perverting the intent of their institution and their society. These individuals are incapable of recognizing any validity in another belief system. With these people controlling the school, there is no possibility of consulting with Indian adults or of treating Indians as equals in the planning of educational experiences for the children. They seldom demonstrate a truly internalized set of values or guiding concepts. Such people often originate in culturally deprived segments of their own society and bear scars from compensating for their own origin. Understanding neither themselves nor their own purposes, much less the institutional purposes of their church, government, or society, the core of the residential school operating personnel can fall back upon only the pecking order-mechanisms of very primitive social organizations. Inherent in their closed belief systems are perceptions of hostility everywhere, a universe in which one must fight for the slightest recognition, a population with base and sinful motivations, and the capacity to achieve ultimate personal gratification only by the means of identifying one's self with the highest possible authority.

The provision of such personnel for the school is not surprising, although it may well be called disgraceful in an affluent society. It is not the "fault" of the church; it would be an unusual institution of any kind which did not seek to perpetuate itself. Given the great amount of power delegated to the church by the government, along with the limited funds and rigid routines prescribed by the total educational structure, it is hardly possible to conceive of a sectarian system functioning in any manner other than as it has done.

If change is to come, it will have to begin with the total elimination of sectarian churches from the education of Indians. It must also involve recognition that the education provided at a residential school is provided throughout the school, not just in classroom, and that *all* personnel are teachers. A different type of person is needed at all levels of the school operation, with the best people—in terms of training and of essential humanity—being those who direct the daily lives of the children and, moreover, do this directing as a team. The staff-teacher dichotomy is a function of organizational self-preservation and is abortive of a unified goal-directed set of activities. The teachers must function as a single group to identify the needed learnings among Indian children and to provide the diversity of experiences which will enable Indian children to achieve a self-expanding awareness of themselves as individuals of worth in their total society (including especially their school life).

Beyond the school changes are needed in governmental attitudes and efforts, if Indians are to acquire truly functional roles as members of Canadian society. The artificial, arbitrary imposition of a separate legalized status to Indians must end. Instead of being forced into a separate identity, Indians must be involved in community processes to the end that they acquire positive community identity. It is too late to achieve this easily, as might have once been done, but it can still be achieved provided Indians are permitted to be involved in the decision-making about events important to *them* with assurance that their decisions will have the same weight as those of the Whiteman and that they will be permitted to cope with the consequences of such decisions as does the Whiteman, without arbitrary ultimate authority intervening.

What better place to begin this process than in relation to schooling? Residential schools may continue to be a necessity for many years in the vast, sparsely settled northern regions. If so, they will be as great a necessity for isolated (or broken) Whiteman families as for Indian families. Local communities, including Indians and Whitemen together, should make the decisions of who does and who does not attend residential schools, not the welfare-state authorities. Similarly, decisions about the curriculum, the organization, and the personnel of residential schools could and should involve all members of the community, undifferentiated and jointly communicating to fulfill their perceived needs.

Such a process can no longer be expected to "just happen." Community therapy would be required which, in turn, would require trained community workers and a massive restructuring of the government and the Canadian social order. It may be utopian to consider such possibilities, but it is not an exaggeration to point out the likely unhappy consequences of failure to make a massive effort to change the present patterns. The Indian population will *not* disappear as fatuous Whitemen once believed. It is the most rapidly growing ethnic group in Canada. The American Indian, like the American Negro, is the Whiteman's creation—a creation conceived in error and developed by a ghastly series of compounded errors. Today the Whiteman is reaping the bitter harvest of his errors in relation to the Negro. Every year of failure to attempt to rectify Indian errors brings closer the possibility of a similar harvest.

References

ANASTASI, ANNE, 1960, *Differential Psychology.* New York: Crowell-Collier and Macmillan, Inc.

BALIKCI, ASEN, 1963, *Vunta Kutchin Social Change.* Ottawa, Ont.: Government of Canada, Northern Coordination and Research Centre, Department of Northern Affairs and National Resources.

BRITISH COLUMBIA PROVINCIAL GOVERNMENT, 1960, *Programme of Studies for the Elementary Schools of British Columbia,* Vol. 1, Primary Grades; Vol. 2, Intermediate Grades. Victoria, B.C.: Provincial Department of Education.

COHEN, RONALD, 1962, *An Anthropological Survey of Communities in the Mackenzie-Slave Lake Region of Canada.* Ottawa, Ont.: Government of Canada, Northern Coordination Research Centre, Department of Northern Affairs and National Resources.

GOVERNMENT OF CANADA, *The Indian Act, Office Consolidation* (of Revised Statutes of Canada, Chapter 149 as amended by 1952–1953; Chapter 41; and 1956, Chapter 40). Ottawa, Ont.: Department of Citizenship and Immigration.

———, 1961, *Report of Indian Affairs Branch for the Fiscal Year Ended March 31, 1961.* Reprinted from the Annual Report of the Department of Citizenship and Immigration. Ottawa, Ont.: The Queens Printer.

HAVIGHURST, R. J., and B. L. NEUGARTEN, 1955, *American Indian and White Children; A Sociopsychological Investigation.* Chicago, Ill.: University of Chicago Press.

JENNESS, DIAMOND, 1957, *The Indians of Canada.* Bulletin No. 5, Anthropological Series No. 15. Ottawa, Ont.: National Museum of Canada.

KING, A. RICHARD, 1964, "A Case Study of an Indian Residential School." Unpublished Ph.D. dissertation, Stanford University (also available in microfilm).

KRAUSE, AUREL, 1848, *The Tlingit Indians: Result of a Trip to the Northwest Coast of America and the Bering Straits.* Seattle, Wash.: University of Washington Press. Translated by Erna Gunther, 1956.

LEWIS, OSCAR, 1961, *The Children of Sanchez.* New York: Random House, Inc.

OSGOOD, CORNELIUS, 1936, *Contributions to the Ethnography of the Kutchin.* Yale University Publications in Anthropology, No. 14. New Haven, Conn.: Yale University Press.

RAY, CHARLES E., 1958, *A Program of Education for Alaska Natives.* Fairbanks, Alaska: University of Alaska.

YUKON TERRITORIAL GOVERNMENT, 1962, *Manual for Yukon Teachers.* Whitehorse, Y.T.: Territorial Department of Education.

Recommended reading

GODDARD, PLINY, 1916, *The Beaver Indians.* Anthropological Papers of the American Museum of Natural History, Vol. 10.

——, 1926, *Similarities and Diversities within Athapaskan Linguistic Stocks.* Proceedings, International Congress of Americanists, Part 2.

In this book, one of the earliest anthropological studies of the Indians of the Northwest Territories and the Yukon, Goodard portrays much of the indigenous culture and supplies insights into the changes resulting from Indian contact with Whiteman.

GOVERNMENT OF CANADA, 1959, *The Canadian Indian;* and

——, 1960, *Indians of British Columbia.* Ottawa, Ont.: Indian Affairs Branch, Department of Citizenship and Immigration.

Both documents are factual surveys of the current status of Indians along with statements of the Canadian government's policies in dealing with Indians.

——, 1960, *Guidance Manual for Indian Schools.* Ottawa, Ont.: Indian Affairs Branch, Department of Citizenship and Immigration.

A manual intended for the use of all who teach Indian students. Well planned and well stated.

——, 1961, *Minutes and Proceedings and Evidence, Joint Committee of the Senate and the House of Commons and Indian Affairs.* Senator James Gladstone, Chairman. Ottawa, Ont.: The Queens Printer.

A series of pamphlets containing verbatim accounts of the committee proceedings, interviews with Indian representatives from all over Canada, and reports by government officials. A document in broad perspective of the peripheral nature of the Indian's place in American—and Canadian—society.

HONIGMAN, JOHN J., 1949, *Culture and Ethos of Kaska Society.* Yale University Publications in Anthropology, No. 40. New Haven, Conn.: Yale University Press.

An insightful reconstruction of the indigenous cultural patterns of the Indians of the region—although no "Kaska" Indians, as such, could be found in 1962.

KROEBER, ALFRED, 1947, *Cultural and Natural Areas of Native North America.* Berkeley: University of California Press.

The most authoritative and reliable source for identifications of broad groups or Indian populations.

MACNEISH, JUNE HELM, 1961, *The Subsistence Economy of the Dogrib Indians of Lac LaMartre in the Mackenzie District of Northwest Territories.* Ottawa, Ont.: Government of Canada, Northern Coordination and Research Centre, Department of Northern Affairs and National Resources.

An ethnographic study of subsistence patterns very similar to those of the traditional Yukon Indians, particularly in regard to technology, uses of flora and fauna, and general "bush" life.

——, 1962, *The Lynx Point People: A Northern Athabascan Band.* Ottawa, Ont.:

Government of Canada, Northern Coordination and Research Centre, Department of Northern Affairs and National Resources.

A charming, accurate, and intimate account of isolated Indian community life.

MORICE, REV. A. G., 1910, *History of the Catholic Church in Western Canada.* Toronto, Ont.: The Musson Book Company, Ltd.

A naturally partisan, but accurate—or believable—account of early missionary activity of this group.

RENAUD, REV. ANDRE, 1958, *Indian Education Today.* Anthropologica 6. Ottawa, Ont.: Research Centre for Amerindian Anthropology.

Father Renaud, an Oblate priest, reports on his broad study of Indian residential schools. This is the only substantial research as yet done in Canada on the subject.

VAN STONE, JAMES W., 1963, *The Snowdrift Chipewyan.* Ottawa, Ont.: Government of Canada, Northern Coordination and Research Centre, Department of Northern Affairs and National Resources.

Along with Balikci, Cohen, and MacNeish, Van Stone contributes insights into the adaptations of northern Indians as modern, technological developments surge around them. These are among the very few available accounts of present conditions. The Department of Northern Affairs and National Resources is far ahead of any other Canadian organization in effecting social research in arctic and subartic Canada.

CASE STUDIES IN EDUCATION AND CULTURE

GENERAL EDITORS
George and Louise Spindler

THE NEW MATHEMATICS AND AN OLD CULTURE:
A Study of Learning among the Kpelle of Liberia
John Gay, Cuttington College, Liberia
Michael Cole, University of California, Irvine

THE SCHOOL AT MOPASS: A Problem of Identity
A. Richard King, USAID, Teachers College—Columbia

NICHU: A Jàpanese School
John Singleton, University of Pittsburgh

EDUCATION IN REBHAUSEN: A German Village
Richard A. Warren, Stanford University

A KWAKIUTL VILLAGE AND SCHOOL
Harry F. Wolcott, University of Oregon

Related Series Edited by George and Louise Spindler
CASE STUDIES IN CULTURAL ANTHROPOLOGY
STUDIES IN ANTHROPOLOGICAL METHOD

HOLT, RINEHART AND WINSTON, INC.
383 Madison Avenue, New York, N.Y. 10017